YOUNG LEARNERS
AND THE
MICROCOMPUTER

YOUNG LEARNERS
AND THE
MICROCOMPUTER

Daniel Chandler

OPEN UNIVERSITY PRESS
Milton Keynes

Open University Press
A *division of*
Open University Educational Enterprises Limited
12 Cofferidge Close
Stony Stratford
Milton Keynes MK11 1BY, England

First published 1984

British Library Cataloguing in Publication Data

Chandler, Daniel
Young learners and the microcomputer.
1. Education, Elementary—England—Data
processing   2. Microcomputers—England
I. Title
372.16'7   LB1028.43

ISBN 0–335–10579–3
ISBN 0–335–10578–5 Pbk

Text design by W.A.P.
Cover design by Paul Clark

Printed and bound in Great Britain
at the Alden Press, Oxford

Contents

For Robin and Rowen

Preface

Thinking about the computer's role in education does not mean thinking about computers, it means thinking about education.

Alan Ellis[1]

This book was written for all who share a concern for young children's learning and the social impact of technology. It was written for parents as well as for teachers, not simply so that they might learn something about how schools are using computers, but in order to heighten awareness of an increasingly important role for computers in relation to children's learning in the home. Writing for parents as well as teachers has allowed me to concentrate on educational rather than administrative issues, which may also make it more interesting to teachers. As one group of teachers politely suggested when listening to some early readings, this book is not about computers but about education.

One can hardly explore the use of computers as a medium without discussing what we are learning by using them. This discussion need have nothing to do with 'teaching', or even 'education'. Fortunately, the computer was not designed as a piece of 'educational technology' for schools: it was designed far more broadly as a tool for extending our intellectual capabilities. Schools which consider the issue in terms of simply absorbing computers into the curriculum are tending either to reject their use altogether because they do not fit neatly into the curriculum, or are attempting to use them simply as supportive 'teaching machines' and consequently trivializing their potential for learning. The issue of whether or not to introduce computers into schools is, however, leading some to think again about the adequacy of curricula. Perhaps one of the most valuable effects of the appearance of microcomputers in schools has been to generate discussion about such matters as the nature of learning, children as thinkers, our concepts of 'childhood', issues of control, and the future of educational institutions. As a polemical essay into the field rather than an academic treatise I hope this book will help to keep such discussions alive.

1984 – the year of this book's publication – could herald an Orwellian battle for the control of the mind. Children will be kept under control by computers unless we take positive steps to ensure that instead, children learn to control them. This is not to suggest a conscious conspiracy against children by teachers and parents, most of whom would wish only that children should extend their capabilities as learners. Apart from the motivation of commercial interests to produce passive consumers rather than thinkers, probably the main reason for the scarcity of imaginative software and applications has been popular ideas about what computers are like. These ideas have already had a profound effect on our attitude to education.

When the human brain is thought of as a computer, then: children tend to be treated as information-handling systems rather than as explorers; learning is reduced to data-capture rather than a search for meaning, measured in terms of quantifiable output rather than observed as understanding; thought is presented as information-processing rather than the play of creative intelligence; language is reduced to a communication system, and its personal use for examining thoughts and feelings ignored; reading in schools becomes the passive assimilation of data rather than an active and pleasurable pursuit; writing is treated as a means of storing data rather than a tool for thought; and education comes to mean the institutional imposition of instructional programmes rather than the maintenance of appropriate opportunities for learning by doing (and, as David Holbrook once said, by *being*).

The unconscious reductionism of this abuse of language would lend itself well to political manipulation, as George Orwell foresaw:

> Newspeak was designed not to extend but to *diminish* the range of thought . . . The special function of certain Newspeak words . . . was not so much to express meanings as to destroy them.[2]

Whatever the usefulness of the computer metaphor to cognitive scientists, imagery derived from the use of computers is tending to narrow popular models of thinking and learning. This need not continue to be so: becoming conscious of the imagery is a stage in preventing it from dictating the way we think. Real understanding of what computers can and cannot do will help us to dispel the myth that computers operate like the human brain and that we are simply unreliable computers. Isaac Asimov once coined the phrase 'the Frankenstein complex' to describe the unreasoning distrust of our own technological creations. Adopting a Luddite position and opposing technology *per se* is no answer. Active involvement with technology is essential if the myth is not to triumph, but it must be an involvement which involves the conscious exercise of our critical faculties, for as the media scholar Marshall McLuhan wrote, 'We are all robots when uncritically involved with our technologies'.[3]

WORDS OF THANKS

It would take many pages to list the names of all those whose advice and assistance has enriched this book, directly or indirectly. I thank them all, but I hope I will be forgiven for listing only a token few. In defence of those named I would point out that this does not necessarily represent an endorsement of the perspective I have chosen to adopt.

Anthony Adams; Professor Les Blackwell; Marion Blake; Mary Bothwell; Stephen Butler; Don Clark; Tom Day; Professor Wallace Feurzeig; Andrew Fluck; Alan Greenwell; Eleanor Hardt; Professor Ulrich Hardt; Mallory Heatley; Julie High; John Holt; Esmor Jones; Dr Hal Jorgenson; Dr Glenn Kleiman; Julie Ann Kniskern; Professor Marvin Klein; Dr Jim Levin; Liz and Trevor Lusty; Rachel Marcus; Dr Stephen Marcus; Kim O'Driscoll; Dr Henry Olds; Phyllis Reynolds; Andee Rubin; Patrick Scott; Dr Mike Sharples; Scott Sizemore; Dr Carl Smith; Professor Frank Smith; Jan Stewart; Rob Weedon; and David Zacchei.

I could not have obtained access to the printed materials I have consulted without the cooperation of the following libraries: the Gutman Library at the Harvard Graduate School of Education; the Education Library at McGill University, Montreal; the Reading Room of the MIT Laboratory for Computer Science; the Professional Library of the Portland Public Schools in Oregon; Wheelock College Library in Boston, Massachusetts; the British Library; the Jennie Lee Library at the Open University, Milton Keynes; the library of the Education Department at the University of Cambridge; and the CEDAR collection at Imperial College, University of London.

My tour of the United States and Canada would have been quite impossible without the generous financial assistance provided by the Specialist Tours Department of the British Council in London, and the kind support of the Council's representatives in Canada and the USA. Special thanks to Western Washington University for their generosity in arranging a private flight into Canada.

The book was written and prepared for typesetting using a BBC Microcomputer system with a VIEW word-processing chip provided by David Johnson-Davies of Acornsoft. The index was compiled using a sorting program specially written by David Butler.

Finally, I thank those who have provided me with the kind encouragement and gentle criticism which has sustained me: Rose Chandler, David Butler and my patient editor, John Skelton.

Note: Throughout the text, the pronoun 'she' has been adopted as literary convenience, and should be taken to include the male.

Daniel Chandler
November 1983

Acknowledgements

The author and publisher would like to thank the following for permission to reproduce copyright material: Byte Publications, Inc. for the cartoon from 'The Generic Word Processor' by Philip Schrodt, appearing in the April 1982 issue of BYTE magazine, copyright © 1982 Byte Publications, Inc.; Kay-Gee-Bee Music and Monty Python for an abridged transcription of the Thomas Hardy sketch from Monty Python's *Matching Tie and Handkerchief* (Charisma Records catalogue number CAS 1080), copyright © 1973 Kay-Gee-Bee Music Ltd; Robert Lawler for permission to use an extract from his article in the June 1982 issue of *The Boston Review*.

1

A Mechanical Instructor?

'That's the reason they're called lessons,' the Gryphon remarked: 'because they lessen from day to day.'

Lewis Carroll[1]

The microcomputer is a tool of awesome potency which is making it possible for educational practice to take a giant step backwards into the nineteenth century. It has arrived just in time to delay the emergence of schools into a 'post-industrial' society (which was itself heralded by the appearance of the early mainframe computers). And it is the ultimate weapon of those who want to get 'back to the Basics', allowing them to process children from 'input' to 'output' in terms of 'behavioural objectives' and 'quality control'. A vast new range of commercial interests is competing to meet the demand. Crude behaviourism in a seductive new guise has dominated the educational software market in North America and (to a lesser extent) Britain since the appearance of the personal computer in 1975.

Many primary and elementary school teachers in Britain and North America are using microcomputers in the interests of 'progress' or 'modernity'. The most imaginative and sensitive teachers may easily become so overwhelmed by the pressure to use computers or so mesmerized by the technology that when they use the computer in the classroom they may come to inflict on their charges mechanistic exercises which they would otherwise have condemned with vigour. One primary teacher from the North of England declared that her use of the computer in her classroom provided 'a modern, exciting way of practising times tables which saves children chanting them'.[2] She did not question the logic of using a sophisticated and powerful medium for such a purpose (still less the educational value of rote learning).

Others have been conditioned to regard computers as more 'efficient' than they are. The shortcomings of existing methods of teaching the '3 Rs' need no longer be blamed on the methods when even the teachers are prepared to blame themselves, allowing computers to administer instructional programmes they have sometimes been too human to operate. The head teacher of an English primary school advises that, 'No teacher can compete . . . [with] the speed with which the computer can tell the child if his solution is correct'.[3]

'Isn't that marvellous', declared one primary teacher trying to teach word-recognition, 'I can tell them once or twice, and that computer can tell them another ninety-eight times'.[4] And, adds a primary head teacher: 'The computer can be asking a child the same question at the end of the day that it was asking at the beginning of a day . . . It does not tire of the child who cannot get the answer right'.[5] This particular way of using computers exhibits what such teachers call 'patience'. If they were on the receiving end, I suspect they would be more likely to call it something else. A 7-year-old American boy who pressed inappropriate keys in a program of mathematics drill was treated to the message 'Stop it!' on both sides of the screen. He grumbled, 'You don't have to tell me twice', and later wanted to know what else the computer was watching and if it was going to tell on him.[6]

Well might he ask. One deputy head teacher in a Merseyside junior school observed that 'most children enjoy having to solve problems within set times. There are more subtle uses however,' he continues, without any indication of the Big Brotherly implications of such possibilities: ' An example is the check that can be kept on how long a child is taking to respond to questions'.[7] As the use of computers in schools continues to increase, the ease of 'monitoring' users will mean that in many schools there will be increasingly more testing and record-keeping, or as Frank Smith puts it, "quality control' of both the learner and the teacher, no matter how insignificant the mistake or irrelevant the learning task'.[8]

Computers are presented as offering 'individualized tuition' or, more incautiously, 'a personal tutor'. The most famous champion of this use of computers – Patrick Suppes of the Computer Curriculum Corporation – declared that 'one can predict that in a few more years millions of school children will have access to what Philip of Macedon's son Alexander enjoyed as a royal prerogative: the personal services of a tutor as well-informed and responsive as Aristotle'.[9] Advocates point to the way in which the computer can be programmed to ask a user for her name, and to employ this during use as if in conversation. In fact children themselves quickly tire of this ploy. Others observe that 'students move as quickly or as slowly as they want',[10] which by Orwellian doublethink is sometimes referred to as giving children 'control of the learning process' (no doubt just as allowing Socrates to decide when to take the hemlock gave him control of the dying process). Sometimes the 'level' of the program can be set, usually in advance by the teacher. In practice, the framework remains exactly the same, with variations in examples which have been set by the programmer according to preconceptions of his own about their relative 'difficulty'. As Professor Jim Howe and Dr Ben du Boulay at the University of Edinburgh's Department of Artificial Intelligence put it, 'individualized instruction' would appear to mean 'that each pupil gets individual access to the program rather than specific teaching that takes his individual strengths and weaknesses into account'.[11]

The range of software which can be described as 'tutorial applications' is considerable. At one end of the spectrum there is a small but growing amount of sophisticated software, usually dealing with a very restricted content area (such as subtraction), in which an attempt is made to identify what kind of reasoning the users are applying and to adopt strategies to match them; at the other end of the spectrum are the bulk of commercial programs which do little more than act as electronic page-turners. Tutorial applications constituted nearly eighty per cent of the programs found in one of the major catalogues of educational software in North America, as Figure 1 shows.[12] No similarly extensive catalogue of British software exists at present, so it would be difficult to compile a similar chart, but reading the Software Shortlist in the magazine *Educational*

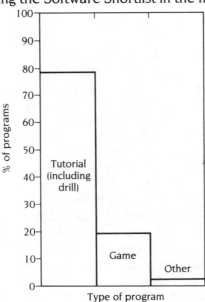

Figure 1 Compiled from the *School Microware Directory*, Spring 1982, Dresden Associates, Dresden, Maine

Computing will reveal that although the pattern is less pronounced, a large percentage of commercial software in Britain is still teacher-centred.

In fact, explicitly instructional programs generally in use in primary and elementary schools are usually little more than drills and tests. A flavour of these programs is provided in this review – by an English Middle School headteacher – of a spelling program:

> This program provides graded exercises in the spelling of a wide variety of English words. The program has a number of levels – 5 in all, giving graded practice at varying levels of difficulty.
>
> I liked very much the idea behind the program. You are tested 20 times in a session and each time you are given four spellings for each word and asked which one is spelt correctly. You then have to type in the spelling of the one you think to be correct. The author has chosen his words well and his 'mistakes' or wrongly-spelt words reflect common errors of children.
>
> The program has some useful features worthy of note. To let you know when an input is expected you are told by a flashing cursor, and a nice flashing sequence is used to tell you if you are right or wrong. I *do like programs that summarize at the end of the session the things you have done wrong* [my emphasis]. This program does this too.
>
> After a months' use in school across the Middle School age-range (around 9-13 in Britain) they seemed bug-free, crash-proof and kid-proof even when all sorts of answers and attempts to make illegal entries were made.[13]

Aside from the bad practice of presenting (and thus reinforcing) misspelt words, it is extraordinary that any set of pre-selected words should be regarded as reflecting 'common errors of children' *en masse*. The declaration that 'the author has chosen his words well' would appear to mean that it is hoped that children will spell most of them inaccurately. The 'features' in the program's presentation considered 'worthy of note' consist of the cursor (a little line) flashing to tell the child when to respond, and the use of flashing to indicate the adequacy of the response, hardly inspiring even in the drill-and-practice genre, and guaranteed to bore the child who was already competent at spelling and dispirit the child whose failure is advertised to her peers. After all these remarks it should perhaps come as no surprise that the teacher considers it to be of positive value to remind children of their failure. In this context the observation that the program seemed 'crash-proof' and 'kid-proof' suggest that this teacher regards computers as instruments of infallible authority, and this perception seems finally confirmed when one realizes that the computer is clearly a police officer, ever alert for 'illegal entries'.

'Give them the worst-presented and dreariest maths or language practice,' observes one reporter, 'and there's something about the machine, or the instant feedback, or the comfortable (and misguided) feeling that no teacher is assessing and controlling the work, that makes children stick to the task'.[14] For those obsessed with 'work', 'standards' and 'the Basics' the question of what is being learnt is far less important than that children should 'stick to the task'. The victims are seduced into doing so with gratuitous sounds and graphics, and, for a medium frequently described as 'non-judgemental', there is an extensive use of crude 'rewards' in terms of 'scores' or trivial games. Teachers only too conscious of 'accountability' can be all too ready to swallow with delight advertisements which cite 'statements by astonished teachers whose students began asking for extra time at math or language drill or whose short attention spans were suddenly transformed. Reports of students having to be pried away from computers and of performance levels increasing dramatically are almost commonplace'.[15]

A dramatic but logical extension of this view is vividly expressed by Arthur C. Clarke:

> It would be hard to think of any invention that would be more valuable than the device which science-fiction writers have called a Mechanical Educator. As depicted by authors and artists, this remarkable gadget usually resembles the permanent wave machine of a ladies' hair-dressers' [sic] and it performs a rather similar function – though on the material *inside* the skull . . . The Mechanical Educator could impress on the brain, in a matter of a few minutes, knowledge and skills which might otherwise take a lifetime to acquire. A very good analogy is the manufacture of a gramaphone record; the music may have taken an hour to perform, but the disc is stamped out in a fraction of a second, and the plastic 'remembers' the performance perfectly.[16]

My rejection of the philosophy underlying such visions is, I hope, evident. One objection is that this passive process makes a child regard learning as rather like consuming a 'take-away' snack: it's pre-cooked and pre-packaged – all you need to do is open the package and consume it. Clarke clearly regards learning as consisting of memorizing things, believes that we find it difficult to do this, and would therefore be delighted if we could get the process over with as quickly as possible. Whilst this may be a fair description of the impression with which schooling leaves many people, real learning is not like this at all.

We all learn effortlessly most of the time without being conscious of doing so. When we reflect on our experiences we can recall a host of details which we had not tried to commit to memory, sometimes from many years ago. Most of us are also successful when we *try* to learn if we enjoy the activity. Learning only becomes difficult when it is reduced to the deliberate assimilation of facts. It is made even more difficult when somebody else is telling you what, when and how you must learn. One of the saddest results of schooling is that many people come to regard learning and thinking as activities alien to them. As one saying has it, children enter school as question-marks, and leave as full-stops, their natural curiosity and delight in discovery crushed.

Even if this use of computers succeeds in force-feeding children with facts or 'skills', what does it teach them about learning? It could hardly be more effective in teaching children that learning is a passive, atomistic and convergent activity. The bar-chart shown in Figure 2 illustrates a typical trend in the bulk of educational software to fragment and decontextualize learning. In this breakdown of a range of software for the language arts, the tendency is clearly to narrow the child's focus in relation to text.[17]

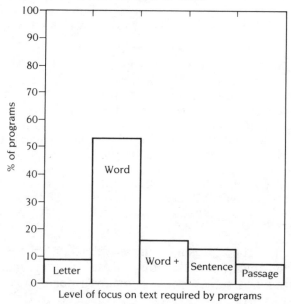

Level of focus on text required by programs

Figure 2   Compiled from the *School Microware Directory*, Spring 1982, Dresden Associates, Dresden, Maine

Such a use of computers makes 'learning' a disjointed and trivial ritual which children may justly perceive as having nothing to do with them: a celebration of futility. It encourages automatic conformism and the need for directives which are followed without thought and without question: exactly those qualities which would make children obedient members of a society in which 'freedom is slavery' and 'ignorance is strength' as in George Orwell's nightmare vision of *Nineteen Eighty-Four*.

With all the talk of 'diagnosis', 'monitoring' and 'remediation', the use of computers for programmed instruction and drill-and-practice constitutes a hospital model of learning, with children automatically regarded as sick patients, learning as receiving treatment, and computer programs used as potent drugs, with the prescriptions dispensed by administrators and commercial interests, leaving teachers, as we are often told, 'free to attend (like nurses) to the more personal needs of their charges'. Jonathan Swift had an answer for those seeking more effective ways of dispensing education as medicine:

> I was at the Mathematical School, where the Master taught his Pupils after a Method scarce imaginable to us in Europe. The Proposition and Demonstration were fairly written on a thin Wafer, with ink composed of a Cephalick Tincture. This the student was to swallow upon a fasting Stomach . . .
> As the Wafer digested, the Tincture mounted to his Brain, bearing the Proposition along with it. But the Success hath not hitherto been answerable . . . partly by the Perverseness of Lads; to whom this Bolus is so nauseous, that they generally steal aside, and discharge it upwards before it can operate . . .[18]

We do not have to endure the medicalization of learning, still less do we need to accept that, in the interests of 'objectivity' or efficiency, this is where technology must lead. It involves not only a disabling of the child, but also the trivialization of what could be a powerful tool for the learner.

In the hospital model of learning the control of the activity resides with the program designer, whose framework is forever frozen in the program. To liberate the user and to extend the potential of the computer as a tool we need to shift the locus of control, so that far more control resides with the user than with the system she is using. At the opposite end of this hypothetical spectrum the user is able to create the framework for herself. Figure 3 illustrates a range of computer uses for young learners, with the hospital model on the left representing the locus of control as lying close to the program, and the workshop model on the right in which control lies far closer to the user. The intervening models represent intermediate stages, though the divisions (and consequently even the sequence) should not be taken as clear-cut. The particular applications explored in this book will serve to provide a flavour of the variety of creative uses for computers in education, introducing games and simulations, word-processing, information handling and programming. The examples chosen hardly exhaust the possibilities but they may help to suggest the range of alternatives. Ultimately the only limitation is our breadth of vision, which governs our assumptions about what both children and computers can do.

THE LOCUS OF CONTROL

Program ←——————→ User

Tutorial	Games	Simulation games	Experimental simulation	Content-free Tools	Programming languages
Programmed Instruction Drill and practice	Computer as player or referee	Computer as game-world: eg. Empire-style games and the ADVENTURE genre	Mathematically based models of processes such as scientific experiments	word-processors sound and graphics manipulators databases scientific instruments control technology	Logo BASIC Smalltalk
Hospital Model: User as Patient	Funfair Model: User as Emulator	Drama Model: User as Role-player	Laboratory Model: User as Tester	Resource Centre Model: User as Artist or Researcher	Workshop Model: User as Inventor

2

The learning game

'No, no! The adventures first,' said the Gryphon in an impatient
tone: 'explanations take such a dreadful time.'

Lewis Carroll[1]

Playful learning

All of us, not just children, learn more effectively when we are at our
most 'playful': when we are actively participating in an enjoyable
experience, or when we engage with ideas in a way which involves
the exercise of our own creativity. For the young child far more
learning occurs during play than in any deliberate and structured
manner. It is through the experience and language of play that
young children naturally make sense of the world. They are not
conscious of their activity as 'learning': the adult distinction between
doing and learning means nothing to them. Indeed, it need hardly
be regarded as a coincidence that most children tend to lose their
interest in *thinking* at the same time as they are made to feel that
playing is 'only for children', and that what they should be doing is
'working' (which is used by both parents and teachers as a synonym
for learning). In schooling systems, this process is usually largely
complete by the time children reach the age of 12, by which time all
the richness of language and thought which finds expression in play
can be outlawed and then buried by the individual for ever. Whilst
teachers of young children are not, of course, unmindful of the
importance of play in children's learning, even in the earliest years
of schooling many teachers habitually make distinctions between
'play' and the 'real work' towards which they hope children will
'progress'.[2] Catherine Garvey lists some of the characteristics of
play: it is spontaneous, voluntary and enjoyable; it actively involves
the participant, and it has no extrinsic goals.[3] It is hardly surprising

that it cannot survive in a curriculum. Even 'dramatic improvization' rarely captures the free but fragile spirit of play, which is gradually eroded by institutionalization.

Games remain, of course. But as Iona and Peter Opie observe, 'Play is unrestricted, games have rules.'[4] Various kinds of games are a feature of the activities of children during the years of primary schooling, and teachers of course utilize them to some extent as an educational technique. Constrained as they are, even games of this kind retain a potential to stimulate playful learning. But it is worth noting that they usually bear little comparison with the street games of children, where, as the Opies point out, children 'seldom need an umpire, they rarely trouble to keep scores, little significance is attached to who wins or loses, they do not require the stimulus of prizes... Indeed children like games in which there is a sizeable element of luck, so that individual abilities cannot be directly compared'.[5] A competitive strain, does, of course, enter into children's own games as they get older: indeed, part of their function may be to help them to rehearse strategies for survival in a competitive society. However, the greatest value of games in a changing world is that they demand adaptive behaviour, and if adults are to make any positive contribution towards future-focused learning we need to participate with children in games in which tolerance and trust are accorded value.

Games can be a great leveller: one of their great advantages may be the rare opportunity which they offer for adults as well as children to enjoy participating in an activity on equal terms. Games can help parents and teachers to forget for a while some of the unnecessary distinctions which are supposed to divide children from adults, teachers from learners. However, when games involving both adults and children are 'managed' by the adults this particular advantage of the activity is prejudiced from the start. Computers will not replace the physical experience of playing Grandmother's Footsteps or the social experience of playing 'house'. We would do well to bear in mind Aldous Huxley's warnings of a Brave New World in which 'the Controllers won't approve of any new game unless it can be shown that it requires at least as much apparatus as the most complicated of existing games'. 'Imagine the folly', muses the Director of Hatcheries and Conditioning, 'of allowing people to play elaborate games which do nothing whatever to increase consumption.'[6] Nevertheless, computer-based games may offer us a framework in which the management of some games in schools may be relinquished by the teacher, who, if she wills it, can abandon the roles of rule-maker, referee and expert and can become simply an observant participant. Where teachers or parents are able to adopt such a role (and computers will continue to give children the edge whilst adults are less confident with the technology) children can learn a great deal from the linguistic and social example of the adult, and adults can learn something from the playfulness of children. Alternatively, where teachers feel unable to take on such a non-directive role, the role of the computer, often spoken of as an *administrative* aid to free the teacher of management burdens, could be the *educational* one of freeing the children of the teacher.

Whilst computer-games may stimulate a playful framework for learning, the exploration of computer-based simulations (such as simulations of scientific experiments) may encourage playful thinking, assisting the learner to experiment with hypotheses in ways which can extend her creativity rather than limiting her to the linearity which characterizes formal education. Freed of the intervention of an adult authority-figure preoccupied with managing the activity, children using computer games and simulations may be able to explore shared experiences in talk which is closer to that of the playground than that of the schoolroom, and therefore closer to the language with which they are most comfortable.

Computer games

The most popular (though not necessarily the most common) use of computers in British primary schools is for playing games.[7] This, of course, mirrors the popularity of games on home computers. One American study of children with computers at home found that 88% of those under 12 used them at least in part for playing games (the figures fell to 67% for those over 12).[8]

The use of computer games in the home has been reported to be resulting in increased interaction in the family[9] and, it has been suggested, may be resulting in some fathers taking an increased interest in their children's learning. In primary schools, however, the use of games in which the adult participates as a non-directive player is rare: computer games, for the most part, tend to be used as a reward for compliance or as yet another way of keeping children 'busy'. Very often they seek to exploit the addictive appeal of video arcade games, so that we are seeing the emergence of 'educational' games such as PUNC-MAN and SPELL-INVADERS, which, in the context of school, children may well be more willing to play if the alternative is a 'workcard'. They may be more fun to do, but, aside from the lack of evidence that children learn anything about spelling or punctuation from such games, they ignore the criticism that such activities are as atomistic in their approach to learning as more obviously traditional methods.

Many teachers justify using arcade-style games on the grounds that they believe them to result in 'keyboard confidence', better hand-eye coordination, or even a less passive attitude to the video medium than is the case with television. Even if this is so, one side-effect of this is that as such games tend to be designed by boys for boys, stereotypical masculine values are powerfully reinforced in boys, and can discourage girls from using computers at all. Sara-Louise, just 8 years old, grumbled, 'I think the boys like the computer because of all the space games'. And Gregory Yob has commented that so often what we are presented with is 'another hunt and kill game in an era where mutual cooperation in complex systems is a vital need'.[10] Furthermore, arcade-style computer games promote the myth of 'man versus machine', that primitive psychodrama which we see enacted in the video arcades. Computers are far more than video-game machines, and it is a betrayal of children for teachers to use them in a way which involves little more thought than pressing a door-bell. 'I would make games', declared Colin, a 7-year-old in an English school, 'to make people think harder'.

Games of strategy, logic and analysis do not necessarily require a computer, but the computer can make a major contribution as a manager of complex rules, making it possible for young children to play games which might otherwise have been difficult or impossible.

DEVELOPING TRAY is a computer-based game originally devised by Bob Moy, an advisory teacher with the Inner London Education Authority. To call it a guessing game would be to devalue the *predictive* strategies on which it draws. Essentially, someone (often, but not necessarily, an adult) secretly types a short text (such as a poem), into the computer. The computer then displays it on the screen – but without any letters, so that all one sees are the punctuation-marks. The object of the game is to restore the passage to its original state. The program allows the players to ask for individual letters (or words) to be replaced in the passage automatically, but each request loses them points. On the other hand, as soon as they are able to *predict* a letter or a word they are given points – and the longer their prediction (as with a phrase rather than a word) the more points they score. In fact the reference to scoring is misleading – very few players seem at all interested in the actual score: their sole concern seems to be to reveal the complete text. During the course of the game players use a special 'notepad' feature within the program to record their evolving ideas, which can form a fascinating focus for discussion after the game is over.

Focusing on a complete text the activity has far more value than a HANGMAN game: the players can consider themes as well as letter patterns as the text emerges in the 'developing tray'. With a small group, the game invariably generates animated discussion, as children make and modify hypotheses about the subject of the text. It is an intriguing framework for children to explore a variety of strategies: trying to identify the overall subject, tone and meaning of the text; trying to match the patterns of letters with their knowledge of the patterns of words; looking for links between one concept and another; and predicting words from the form of the phrases. Impulsive and analytical approaches may both have advantages, and in any group children can learn from each other.

Another interesting example is a famous computer program called ANIMAL: a guessing game in which the computer does the guessing.[11] The computer asks for the players to think of an animal and then tries to 'guess' what it might be. It asks questions such as 'Is it an insect?', 'Is it a fish?' and so on. If it fails to guess the animal it asks what the creature is, and then asks for a yes/no question which will distinguish its last guess from the animal the players had been thinking of, e.g. a swallow from an eagle. The computer stores the question for future use, so that with each game, it is 'taught' more by the players. The game is widely used in many versions by children in England and North America. In the following example, three children (A, B and C) aged between eight and nine are playing the game in their lunch-hour at an English school.[12] They are using a version called TREE OF KNOWLEDGE, by Acornsoft, on the BBC microcomputer, and have been 'teaching' the computer about birds.

Screen	Talk
Are you thinking of a bird?	(A): 'Are you thinking of a bird?' CHORUS: Yes. (B): This one's going to be swallow!
Does it live near the sea?	(A): Yes. I know. CHORUS: 'Does it live near the sea?'

(A): N . . . RETURN . . .

Does it hunt by night?

(?): 'Does it . . . ' No.

(A): 'Does it hunt by night?' . . . N . . . RETURN . . .

Does it swoop on its prey?

'Does it swoop on its prey?'

(B): Yes.

(A): Yes . . . Put Y . . .

Does it hover?

RETURN . . .
'Does it hover?' . . .

(B): No . . .

(A): No . . . RETURN . . .

Is it an eagle?

'Is it an eagle?'

(B): No.

(A): N . . . RETURN . . .

What bird are you thinking of?

'What bird are you thinking of?' . . . We're thinking . . .

(B): A swallow!

What bird are you thinking of?
s

(A): A swallow . . .
S . . . S – W . . .

(B): A . . . W – A . . .

(A): Where's . . . Where's . . .

(B): Where's the W?

What bird are you
thinking of?
sw

Now the . . .

(A): A . . . What's next?

(B): L . . . double L . . . 'luh',
'luh' . . . Swall . . .

What bird are you
thinking of?
swall

(A): What's next?

(B): O . . . W . . .

What bird are you
thinking of?
swallow

(A): O . . . W . . .

(B): S . . . S

(A): No, just a swallow.

Right, press RETURN . . .

Please give me a
question to tell the
difference between a
swallow and an eagle.

What's the difference
between swallow and an
eagle?

(B): Swallows . . .

(A): Swallows . . . um . . .

(B): Swallows . . .

(A): What's migrate . . .
migrate?

(B): Swallows go . . .

(?): Look up . . . Look up the
book!

(B): No – swallows go to . . .

(A): What's migrat . . .
[pronounced as in 'migration']

(C): No. Look at the book.
Look at the book.

(A): Yeah, OK. Look for
swallow in the book and it
should say about . . .

(?): Can I borrow . . . ?

(?): Hey right . . .
Swallows . . .

(?): Give it here!

(C): OK. Give it there . . .
There's . . .
Look for swallow.

(B): Swallow in there.

(C): Does . . . Does it . . .

(A): Migrate . . . migrate . . .
migrate . . .

(C): Does it . . .
How d'ya spell. . . ?

(A): Put 'does it. . . ' Put
'does it' in.

(C): Does it . . .

(B): OK . . . D . . . D – No . . .

(A): 'Uzz' . . . [pronounced as in
'does']

(B): 'Duh' . . . O . . .

```
┌─────────────────────────────┐
│                             │
│              D              │
│                             │
│                             │
└─────────────────────────────┘
```

```
┌─────────────────────────────┐
│             Do              │
│                             │
│                             │
└─────────────────────────────┘
```

(C): Do . . . that's 'do' . . .

(B): S . . . E . . .

. . .

(A): E . . . S . . . Does . . . it . . .

Does it

(B): Does it fly away in winter?

(A): No . . . Fly a . . . fly to . . .

(B): Fly to . . . fly away in winter . . .

(A): Fly to hot countries in winter . . .
Does it fly . . .

(B): Away . . . F . . .

(A): Does it fly to hot countries in winter?

(B): That's 'R' I know . . . Need an L, a bent L.

Does it fly

(A): 'Luh' . . . 'Yuh' . . .
(B): 'Y' I need.

(A): There it is . . . Does it fly . . .

(B): A . . .

Does it fly to

(A): to . . .
(B): A . . .

(A): Hot . . .

B): A hot country . . .

(A): Ah, I don't . . . DELETE.

```
┌─────────────────────────────┐
│                             │
│    Does it fly to ah        │
│                             │
│                             │
│                             │
└─────────────────────────────┘
```

(B): A hot . . .

(C): Hot . . .

(?): Space! [referring to
the fact that he hasn't
left a space between words]
. . .
Hot!

(A): No just put DELETE,
DELETE . . .
Right we'll just put hot
countries.

```
┌─────────────────────────────┐
│                             │
│                             │
│    Does it fly to hot       │
│    countries?               │
│                             │
│                             │
└─────────────────────────────┘
```

Where's 'huh'?
(B): To hot countries . . .

. . .

The computer would then go on to ask what the answer to this question would be for the eagle, and would then start a new round (as we began) with, 'Are you thinking of a bird?'.

This transcript has, I hope, served to illustrate the way in which the game proceeds for anyone who may not have seen it in action. Based on it, one can also make an number of observations. The activity, quite unsupervised, is providing a focus for the three boys to learn together in a game framework, despite the obvious differences in their fluency of reading and writing. Its very structured nature results in extraordinary concentration in the interests of accuracy. The need to play together is resulting in player A giving considerable support to player B in spelling words and finding letters on the keyboard. Coming to terms with each other as partners is clearly not always easy, but these children are learning how to cooperate. It has taken them three minutes to decide on a question to distinguish a swallow from an eagle. In the process they have tried to draw information from a book on birds, and have gradually reached a compromise as to the phrasing of the question. In this relaxed setting, their language has been informal enough for them to feel able to think aloud, and tentative offerings have elicited modifications from others. And as each new bird is added, the questions required to distinguish one from another will demand more thought, more consultation with reference sources, more careful phrasing.

One can, of course, play 'Twenty Questions' without a computer: all the computer is doing, after all, is managing the activity. But it easy to underestimate this subtle advantage. Playing the traditional parlour game is very different: although experienced players would narrow the options by moving from more abstract to more concrete questions, the framing of a special question to distinguish one item from another is not necessary: the players are not 'teaching' the controller of the game. The questions do not form a clear framework, and therefore the traditional game tends to be an arena for the experienced to demonstrate their expertise, and little is likely to be learnt about the formulation of questions from simply playing. Where it is played in schools, either the children have to guess the animal the teacher is thinking of, or the teacher manages it as a whole-class activity with children taking turns to think of an animal. In either case, very few children get the chance to say anything, and thinking aloud becomes impossible.

Computer simulation

Just as playing games on a computer can, for particular purposes, have certain advantages over doing so without, so simulations which allow us to explore the effects of particular actions (either through imaginative role-play or the manipulation of mathematical probabilities) can acquire new dimensions when a computer is used. Games and simulations are both systems based on rules. In the case of simulations, however, principles are developed which attempt to mirror aspects of the world. For instance, a simulation of a dairy farm might attempt to incorporate factors reflecting real concerns such as seasonal changes, expenses and disease. This kind of simulation is quite possible without a computer, but if any complexity is required a computer could, once again, make it possible for a far more elaborate simulation to be feasible, particularly for young participants who might otherwise have found the necessary calculations too difficult, distracting or dull.

A program called STEAMROOM has been developed recently in the United States at the Xerox Research Centre in Palo Alto. It is a working model of the boiler system used to generate steam in large ships, and offers an initial training-ground for those who will be working in the steamroom on board such vessels.

The program allows the users to see a screen display of the steamroom from which they can select close-ups of every aspect of the system, right down to single valves. They can be shown animations of the flow of steam through the pipes and boilers under normal conditions, and then can witness the variety of ways in which the system can malfunction. The users can then control the model by opening or closing valves and watching the effects of their actions in perfect safety. Consequently, when they see the real valves and gauges on their ships they will have a far deeper understanding of how the system functions and could have a greater awareness of what kind of options are open to them in order to avert crises.

STEAMROOM is a computer-based simulation program, allowing its users to explore the effect of various strategies on a pre-defined model. It was produced for the US Navy, but Michael Williams, a physicist involved in its development, predicted in 1982 that computer-based models of a similar scale and power would be available to large companies within five years and to schools within ten – a depressingly vivid illustration of the priorities of the industrialized nations.

Although such sophisticated computer-based simulation software is not yet available on home computers, one can already buy a variety of microcomputer programs which come under the broad umbrella of computer simulation, which we may define as 'software in which users can explore the effect of various strategies on pre-defined models of systems'.

In principle, simulation software has many advantages as a learning tool. These may be summarized as follows:

- COST Many scientific experiments would be far too expensive in materials and equipment for all but research institutes to undertake. Less expensive projects might nevertheless be wasteful. The use of computer-based simulations might provide at least some experience of investigating the phenomenon where otherwise the best that could be expected would be watching a filmed version.
- TIME It is often argued that many scientific experiments take far too long for 'learning by discovery' to be practicable, at least within the context of institutional education. Computer-based simulations allow a speeded-up model to be explored, where otherwise more teacher-centred techniques might have been employed.
- SAFETY Some laboratory experiments cannot be undertaken because of the physical danger involved.
- MANAGEABILITY Sometimes models of systems may be too complex to be easy to build or imagine in any way other than on a computer. The microcomputer makes it possible, for instance, for older children to experiment with models of economic

systems, once available only on university mainframe computers.
- HIGHLIGHTING In a computer-based simulation, graphical representations of the changing data can be provided throughout the process, impossible in some chemical experiments in the laboratory. In short, the process can be made easier to understand.
- RE-RUNS The computer makes it easy for users to re-run the simulation as many times as they like in order to experiment with different variable factors and conditions.
- USER CONTROL Where experiments previously impossible are being undertaken, and the variable factors are under the user's control, young learners can take a greater part in controlling the direction of their investigations. They can feel more involved than they would be watching a presentation on film, with a greater sense of being 'on the inside'.
- STIMULUS TO THINKING With the process entirely managed by the computer, users can concentrate more easily on thinking: making hypotheses about why things are happening and speculating about 'what might happen if . . .'. This has been found to be a very effective stimulus to discussion when the activity is undertaken in small groups.
- IN CONTEXT The activities undertaken in simulations make far more sense to young learners than decontextualized exercises focusing on isolated 'skills'.
- AWARENESS OF RELATIVITY The use of computer-based simulations could result in a realization of the importance of variable factors, change, and the particular model involved. Used well, it could lead young learners to remember that 'it all depends . . .'.

Clearly simulation on a computer has many advantages, both as against traditional educational strategies and as compared with the use of computers for drill-and-practice. It is, however, only one tool for inquiry, not a self-sufficient inquiry workshop. In assessing the potential of simulation software we need to bear in mind its limitations as well as its strengths.

Clearly, wherever possible, direct experimentation is clearly more valuable to the learner. Simulating a prism on a computer, for example, would be absurd. Liberating as this use of computers may appear by comparison with traditional teaching methods, simulations can be used badly, so that the learner is still required to 'discover' a 'right answer'. The essentially mechanical nature of the activity may simply be concealed.

Computer-based simulations can be constructed badly so that they grossly oversimplify complex phenomena. Caricatures are sometimes the result of designers attempting to define processes which are not fully understood, and 'educational simulations' may be deliberately simplified in the belief that this makes them easier for children to understand. Computer simulations vary considerably in the degree of subjectivity which underlies their construction and in the range of options offered to users. With a model such as STEAMROOM there can be little argument about the structure of the system and how water is affected by temperature and pressure. However, when dealing with less quantifiable systems the underlying model may be deceptive and misleading, or simply inaccurate. Even more importantly it may be hidden from users, who ought to question its validity but may neither think of doing so nor know how. Simulations of non-scientific phenomena, such as social, economic or historical scenarios can present what Professor Papert has referred to as 'an overly mechanistic view of what society is like'.[13] There is a very real danger that the potency of the medium may result in children absorbing such models as if they were accurate reflections of reality. Such distortions could have subtly dehumanizing effects on the outlook of children on society. The use of computer simulations makes it essential for users to be conscious that the models they use are only personal and selective representations of aspects of the world.

Simulation games / process game?

Some applications of the simulation technique are designed as computer-based games. OREGON TRAIL is a historical simulation game developed in the US (originally at the Minnesota Educational Computing Consortium). It begins: 'This program simulates a trip over the Oregon Trail from Independence, Montana, to Oregon City, Oregon, in 1847. Your family will cover the 2040-mile Oregon Trail in five to six months – if you make it alive.' Imagining themselves as travelling in a covered wagon, players have to make decisions about obtaining food and supplies based on available resources, and must cope with various misfortunes which befall them, such as being bitten by rattlesnakes, breaking legs, having their wagons catch fire and being attacked by bandits. The aim is to involve children in decision-making and problem-solving in a 'realistic' historical context, providing some flavour of what it may have been like to trek to the American west in 1847.

In the UK, a similarly well-known historical variation on the simulation principle is MARY ROSE, produced by Ian Whittington and Barry Holmes (Ginn, 1982). Based on the rediscovery and excavation of King Henry VIII's flagship, the aim is stated as being 'to provide children with the opportunity to find the ship for themselves, to carry out dives on the wreck, to participate in the processes of excavation and research . . . and to share in the exciting business of bringing to life a piece of the past'.[14] Here the object of the activity is to encourage the participants to behave like contemporary archaeologists rather than to take part as actors in a historical drama. The software might be more accurately described as 'computer-managed simulation', since most of the activities in the project (such as using reference books, writing for information and looking at pictorial material) take place away from the computer itself. Whatever the merits of the game may be, the 'excavation' is an abstract process in which no-one gets their hands dirty. The software itself is largely a game-controller which, for instance, tells players whether in their movement around the screen they have stumbled upon part of the wreck. If 'excitement' is a goal, dramatic simulation rather than computer simulation would offer far more than can be achieved by pressing keys.

This last point touches on a potential danger in the genre of computer simulation games as a means of exploring a phenomenon, particularly in view of their popularity: this is that if the activity is largely computer-based, children may learn about how to develop successful strategies for the game without necessarily gaining any deeper understanding of the events being simulated.

Where simulation games are being used in classrooms, teachers need to be clear about whether they are primarily concerned with using a particular game as an enjoyable way of learning about the content, or whether its main value is as a context in which more general thinking strategies can be explored and developed.

If a simulation is used as a content game it can be regarded as no more than a springboard for investigation. Without a great deal of cautious contextualization and imaginative enrichment, OREGON TRAIL could easily be simply an unusual game of dice, and MARY ROSE a game of 'Battleships'. In practice, children need little encouragement to want to find out more from books and other sources when playing such games, but in our delight at their willingness to engage in the acquisition of information we often give a lower priority to their thinking about it. Why did the settlers set out on their daunting trek? What is the significance of the 'finds' recovered from the wreck? An answer sometimes given by teachers to such comments is that they are rather more concerned with the 'process skills' than with the content.

In the case of a simulation program being used as a process game, we need to be sure that it is of practical benefit in developing strategies which empower children as learners. For many teachers who have begun to use computers with children, one of their most exciting discoveries has been the way in which small groups of children can become completely absorbed in a computer-based activity, and begin to talk together about it with real excitement. Sustained, enthusiastic and undirected discussion in which small groups of children spontaneously exchange ideas in relation to officially-sanctioned learning activities, is, after all, rare in schools. As the research of Douglas Barnes, James Britton and Harold Rosen has demonstrated, children learn more effectively when they have the opportunity to make sense of their experiences in their own terms, and when they are relaxed enough, in Rosen's words, to 'trust the tips of their tongues'.[15] Computer-based simulation games have at least the potential to focus discussion on a shared experience without intervening and controlling the shape and language of the discussion as teachers almost invariably do. This is a powerful argument for activities in which small groups use computers together. Additionally, where the teacher is to be an active participant in the activity, simulations offer the particular advantage that there are no 'right answers', only possibilities to be explored together.

We need to ask ourselves what kind of strategies children experiment with, and develop, as players. Early research on 'problem-solving' strategies adopted by children in playing games of this kind,[16] suggests that a major strategy is to make a deliberate attempt to learn from mistakes. Once more, this is a phenomenon common when children use computers in other ways, although the fantasy element and collective responsibility may make such a policy more attractive. Another finding has been that in such games children tend to formulate hypotheses and then try to find supportive evidence for them, rather than being more open-minded and looking for alternative possibilities. Whilst, according to Karl Popper, this is also characteristic of scientists, we may question whether such strategies ought to be challenged rather than reinforced.

Reference is often made to the usefulness of such games in promoting 'decision-making'. But the level of decision-making required can be trivial. The most significant decisions taken by children participating in these simulations in the classroom tend to be in establishing a method of operating as a group. There is certainly a growing body of evidence that the group use of the computer in such activities tends to lead to an increase in collaborative strategies.[17] The development of such an attitude to real-life problem-solving is of course a very necessary part of educating for the future. However, the conscious focus of the games is on decision-making at a less concrete level.

And on what basis are such decisions made? Often they can be

[handwritten margin note:] How do they know?

[handwritten margin note:] See Popper! (Conjec. a Refut.)

made on the basis of little or no evidence at all: wild guesses may be the best policy. It may be argued that it could also be said that many decisions in situations outside school have to be made on the basis of inadequate information. But such decision-making is usually based on a genuine consideration of past experience and of the likely personal or social consequences of an action. In computer-based simulation games the most successful decisions are more likely to be based on deductions players are able to make about the internal logic and mathematics of the software, and these may have little connection with the subtle interplay of cause and effect in reality.

No such problem exists with the genre of ADVENTURE programs: games which 'simulate' an imaginary world. The commercial games, intended to provide 'home entertainment' for a solo player, do have considerable educational potential when used with small groups. Although the original programs were not designed for use by children, many versions which are suitable for children are beginning to become available.

Essentially, players find themselves in locations which are described in words (or sometimes pictures) on the screen. Their goal is to explore the 'landscape' and to solve whatever problems they discover in their travels. This is done by typing in commands to the computer such as 'GO INTO THE ROOM' or 'OPEN THE BOX'.

Such games can stimulate lively discussion as participants experiment with various strategies to solve the situational dilemmas in which they find themselves. Many children find them at least as exciting as arcade-style games. Interesting as ADVENTURE games are, however, the players have no real control over the content of the game: they have to explore a world limited by the imagination of the programmer, which can lead to considerable frustration. The solutions which are required may involve creative 'lateral' thinking but there is usually only one solution to a particular dilemma. Feeling that there was considerable scope here for extending children's capabilities as 'imagineers', in 1980 I began to plan a system which would allow children (and their parents or teachers) to produce their own multi-player ADVENTURE games.

ADVENTURER, which has been programmed by Jan Bright at Chelsea College, does not involve any actual programming on the part of the users. It is an 'authoring system' which prompts the users to provide all the data it needs. A group begins by imagining a scenario and then typing in descriptions of a number of scenes for the action. Next they need to decide on a 'plot' – perhaps seeking a magical ring in a land of giants and dwarfs. The writers need to decide where the players are to begin, and what kind of problems they will have to solve in order to achieve their goal. They can litter the scenes with useful and useless objects such as wands, keys and potions, and can introduce characters other than the players. They must provide the computer with the vocabulary which they wish it to recognize (such as OPEN and DOOR for the players to open doors), and they must 'teach' the computer exactly how to respond to both words and actions. This stage is very demanding, and adult participation is of particular value. During trial runs, the creators will discover the need to improve their original framework until at last the story will be ready to be 'played' by another group, each of whom features as a roving character in the plot.

ADVENTURER won't replace the writing and reading of stories, but in allowing children to create their own story-games it may help them to explore a new form of writing, lessening the gap between games and the written word, and perhaps also making them conscious of the kind of thinking which underlies computer-based models.

This chapter has focused on the usefulness and limitations of computer games and simulations. I have quite deliberately juxtaposed experimental simulations and games. Play is a child's way of discovering the world around her, and as such shares something of the function of research for the scientist. When does playful curiosity become scientific investigation? Perhaps a more playful approach to using computers (not simply giving children computer games to play) could help us to counteract the prevailing bias of the technology, allowing us to celebrate creativity as well as logic.

3

Words which dance in light

Only the hand that erases can write the true thing.
Meister Eckhardt

Computers and literacy

All the enthusiasm about something called 'computer literacy' focuses on the computer and ignores its implications for literacy. By analogy with the concept of 'computer literacy' which seems to form the basis of many recent initiatives in schools, an extra-terrestrial visitor might assume that literacy must consist of learning how to admire the covers of books, how to open them, how to copy a few words, and how to put them carefully back on the shelves. But literacy is a fluent mastery of a medium, allowing one to use it as a tool. Being able to read and write is a powerful advantage for abstract, logical thinking, and extends our capabilities for systematic learning. Therefore, although its character may change, literacy is likely to remain a major asset to most individuals in western society in the foreseeable future.

Children do not, of course, learn to read and write as early or as easily as they learn to talk. The environment in which they grow up is far more supportive of the spoken word than of the written word: we all speak much more than we read or write (linguists have estimated that an 'average' person utters in about two months more words than there are in the whole of Shakespeare!). Although John Holt and Herbert Kohl have argued that children can and ought to learn to read without explicit instruction from adults, and Frank Smith has suggested that the same may be true for writing, all have stressed the critical importance of an environment in which children see that reading and writing are clearly both personally useful and enjoyable.[1] Many children are not lucky enough to experience such conditions often, so that the acquisition of literacy has to become a deliberate effort.

It is easier for children to see a purpose in reading than in writing: they see it going on more often, and will certainly be highly motivated in environments where adults read to, and with, children for pleasure. However, although we are surrounded all the time by writing that most of us can hardly avoid *reading*, most adults do not *write* very much. And when they do, they typically use writing to serve a social purpose which means little to young children: communication with people who aren't there. As Connie and Harold Rosen observe, 'It is easy to think of many reasons why a young child should not want to write and very difficult to think of reasons why he should . . . Why should he want to put on paper (or via paper) what he can so much more easily say directly?'[2]

The computer could play a major part in changing the character and the context of literacy, making it both more accessible and more relevant to young learners. As this chapter will suggest, the editing facilities of word-processing systems make writing physically easier, and the printing capabilities of a good system can make the quality of printed output generated by the youngest user as good as that of a conventionally published book. The comparative ease with which it is possible to use the computer as a writing instrument may help a child to regard writing as less distant from speech. The parent of one 7-year-old boy using a word-processing program called the BANK STREET WRITER observed that 'he wrote more in the way he speaks'. A number of current technological developments could also lessen the gulf which children experience between the spoken and written word. Texas Instruments' *Magic Wand Books* are printed books with a bar-code stripe across the bottom of each page. By passing a bar-code reader over the text a child is able to listen to it being read aloud by a computer-controlled speech synthesizer. Such developments can never rival the physical presence of a story-teller sensitive to her audience as participants, but they could lead children to regard books as more accessible. Other kinds of speech-handling technology may begin to undermine some of the more mundane functions of literacy in everyday life. For instance, some short messages currently using print will be more conveniently replaced with spoken versions (as they already are in some cars). On the other hand (at least until all computers can both reliably decode speech and mellifluously produce it) the range of functions for writing may be extended. People can now write to each other via the telephone system. This may encourage the use of the written word in situations where we currently strain the capabilities of speech (as in giving directions over the phone) or may make possible written activities which had previously not been feasible.

Computers linked via satellite already allow children as far apart as California and Alaska to create an electronic newspaper together, providing both a means and a real purpose for sharing experiences through writing. Dr Jim Levin, a research psychologist at the University of California in San Diego, created a Children's News Service to link children in the tiny Eskimo village of Wainwright (300 miles north of the Arctic Circle) with children in the southern Californian city of La Jolla. Each month the children, between nine and eleven years old, produce a newspaper together using their computers and an 'electronic mail' system. The News Service includes columns for News, Sport, Weather, Fun, Sharing, Life and 'Something Else', with optional advice on how to compose items. The system thus provides not only a medium but a supportive framework for writing. The direct link between children living very different lives provides a real challenge: a Californian child who commented that 'It snowed here in 1967, but I wasn't born yet' must try to communicate with a child like Thommas Aguvluk whose world is 'super cold' and whose food is caribou and whale meat. Consciousness that there is an editorial board at the other end of the line leads the authors to pay particular attention to the revision of their contributions before they finally submit them. In Dr Levin's words, the Children's News Service allows young writers to 'get past the stage of writing as a mechanical act to writing as a communicative act'.

Such factors could have a profound effect on the attitude of young children to the printed word. Consider the example of a three-year-old girl who lives in a household in which the three children have daily access to a computer. Her father makes some thought-provoking observations:

> I began to develop several programs to give Peggy access to the machine . . . Although her general idea of what book reading is may not have changed, she has a different and powerful idea of what reading single words means that derives directly from her experience with computer programs I wrote . . . Her *desire to control the machine* [his emphasis] led her into typing on the computer her first 'written' word . . .
>
> The BEACH microworld [one of the programs he created using the Logo programming language] provides a backdrop for action that can be controlled by the child. Waves and a beach in the foreground, with grass above, and clouds at the top of the display. Against that backdrop, Peggy could create a small picture of an object by specifying a name, then manipulate the picture with commands typed on the computer keyboard. Peggy typically began constructing a scene by typing the word SUN. A yellow circle would appear in the waves. She would raise it up to the sky by keying the word UP repeatedly, change its colour or set it in motion with another word,

and go on to other objects. She could, for example, make a CAR image appear by keying that word, change its location with commands UP, DOWN, MOVE, and specify its heading and velocity with TURN, SLOW, FASTER, and HALT . . . Because the computer can interpret specific words the child does not yet know, she can learn from the computer through her self-directed exploration and experiment . . .

Learning to read from print is necessarily a passive process for the child. Words on the page stand for other people's meanings. Until children start to write they can't use written words for their own purposes. Microcomputers put reading and writing together from the start. A word that Peggy can read is also one she can use to produce on the computer effects that interest her. For Peggy, learning the alphabetic language has become more like what every infant's learning of the vocal language is like.[3]

Here the computer is clearly making literacy both more accessible and more relevant than it usually seems to young children. It is more relevant to the child because she can immediately see an obvious reason for writing and reading. It is more accessible because she is reading what she herself has written rather than something 'locked away' in a book created by someone else. Of course, such accessibility does not necessarily require a computer. But it is also more accessible because writing on the computer requires a far less complex combination of psychomotor functions.

Writing with a computer is easier and more rewarding than writing with a pen. Young children sometimes give surprising reasons why they find this to be so, such as that it doesn't hurt their fingers, that rubbing out doesn't leave a hole in the paper, and that the space-bar allows them to space words evenly. Such declarations are a telling reflection of the considerable physical frustrations which they experience when learning to control a pen. In Frank Smith's words, 'You do not learn to dance wearing heavy boots'.[4] Indeed, when one considers the host of difficulties that young writers have to cope with it is no surprise that some children never learn to write and many more never really exploit the potential of writing.

Peggy, at three years old, is learning to write without using handwriting: the computer, far more than the less flexible typewriter, has shown that handwriting is not an essential part of literacy. Whether they like it or not, schoolteachers are going to have to face the fact that increasing numbers of young children will be entering school having already learned to write using a keyboard without ever having written with a pen or pencil. No doubt handwriting will ultimately become the preserve of artists, as it once was that of monks, the difference being that this time it would have been declined by the majority, rather than withheld from them. Social convenience will continue to require handwriting for special purposes for many years to come, but the computer demonstrates that it need not remain a priority for the young learner.

The comments of Peggy's father also show that this child has discovered the independent existence of words (a quite new insight for a child used only to the continuous flow of speech). She would have become aware of this at a later stage when she came to read printed books, so perhaps there is nothing unusual here except the way in which the discovery has occurred, and the surprisingly early age at which it has happened. In the process, she will also have come to be conscious that the order in which letters appear in a word has some significance: if she doesn't type the letters in the usual order nothing will happen. It is not clear that such a consciousness will be particularly helpful to a child at such an early stage: such low-level consciousness of text might actually hamper a child's freedom of expression.

Far more significantly, she has come to regard the written word as powerful: it can make interesting things happen, sometimes instantly, a phenomenon normally confined to speech. It is therefore possible, as Seymour Papert has suggested, that children using computers may develop 'an *emotional* relationship with alphabetic language different from the relationship most people have'.[5] It is perhaps necessary to point out that it would be sad indeed if, in the delight at a child's joy in discovering words in this way, adults were not to share with them a far wider range of contexts and reasons for using words, but I suspect that it would be very strange for a child with this experience not to want to explore other uses for herself.

An editing tool

It was Graham Wallas who coined the well-known saying, 'How can I know what I think till I see what I say?'. By speaking we may express a thought, by engaging in discussion our friends may help us to pursue some of its implications, but only in writing are we able to stand back, re-examine and re-shape it coolly over a period of time. Its very visibility invites, as it were, a mental magnifying glass, making it potentially a powerful tool of thought. If a child is to use writing as a thinking tool she must at some stage learn to exploit for herself one of the greatest advantages of writing for developing thinking: revising and editing.

Most children do not realize this advantage for themselves, which is perhaps not surprising considering the infrequency with which they are likely to see adults engaged in the process. Another reason is maturational: when young children begin to write they see themselves as making their speech visible. At the very earliest stage of beginning to write they do not edit (although they may ask how to write a word). They are not even conscious of their writing as something to be read, still less of the need to make their meaning clear: they are simply expressing themselves, and may not even expect to read what they have written. Even when the advantages of revising texts are made apparent to them there are many disincentives. If you are writing on paper with a pen and want a neat copy, changing your mind about anything in the text involves rewriting it in its entirety, including passages you may not wish to change at all. As Papert observes, 'for most children rewriting a text is so laborious that the first draft is the final copy, and the skill of rereading with a critical eye is never acquired'.[6] In schools, where neatness is often accorded disproportionate importance, redrafting (where it occurs at all) may therefore tend to be confined to correcting spelling or punctuation rather than reshaping ideas. One American eight-year-old candidly explained his usual strategy when writing in school: 'I write less. Then I have less to recopy.'

Bernard Banet has written that 'the ability to edit a computer-composed product makes the computer an ideal medium for playfully creating, revising and reshaping anything, as one would play with playdough'.[7] The computer is a useful but not, of course, a necessary medium for 'creating, revising and reshaping' text. Children can and do sometimes use a far cheaper word-processing system, consisting of pens, paper, erasers, scissors and paste. Figures 4a – 4d show one wit's portrayal of such a system in the magazine BYTE.[8] These traditional tools have of course far more

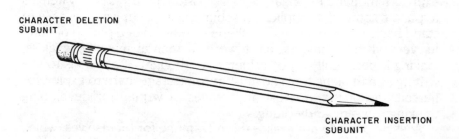

CHARACTER DELETION
SUBUNIT

CHARACTER INSERTION
SUBUNIT

Fig. 4(a): *The GWP System word-processing unit is composed of the character-insertion subunit (at right) and the character-deletion subunit (at left).*

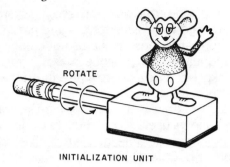

Fig. 4(b): *The word-processing initialization unit, which should be operated over a* *wastebasket.*

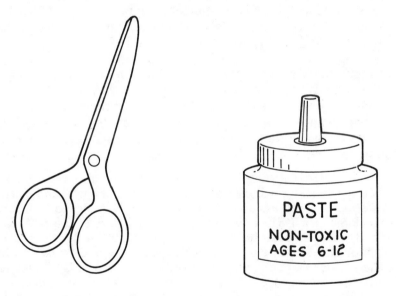

Fig. 4(c): *The block text extraction and replacement units, commonly run in unison.*

SANSKRIT

AMHARIC

HIEROGLYPHICS

Fig. 4(d): *Sample type fonts illustrating the wide variety available with the GWP* *System. The manufacturer claims that if a language can be written, the GWP System* *can be adapted to it.*

flexibility than any computer word-processing system. Children can cut out and rearrange words, sentences and paragraphs in any way they like, with no restrictions on the use of colour and illustrations. But such techniques are in practice messy and tedious, and the activity can quickly become a chore which interferes with the writing process rather than assist it.

A word-processor, or a word-processing program running on a microcomputer, allows users to produce text (on the screen and on paper) which is always legible and attractive. Children know in advance that other people will be able to read it. For many, one of the most liberating discoveries is the DELETE key, each press of which removes completely from the screen the last character typed. Some children in Britain refer to it as the Tippex button (known in the US as White-Out). Secretarial slips can be removed without trace by the writer (or anyone else) as soon as they are noticed. Words, sentences and paragraphs can be shuffled around, inserted or deleted.

Often, children writing with pen and paper in schools start to write, change their minds, and because they don't like to be reminded of what they see as mistakes, cross them out (or screw up the paper) and try again. This is so neatly caught in a satirical sketch by the Monty Python team that I cannot resist the temptation to quote from it:

> COMMENTATOR: And he's off! It's the first word – but it's not a word. Oh no! It's a *doodle* way up on the top of the left-hand margin; it's a piece of *meaningless* scribble. And he's signed his name underneath it. Oh dear, what a disappointing start! But he's off again, and here he goes: the first word – at 10.35 on this very lovely morning. It's three letters; it's the definite article; and it's '*the*'! . . . But he's crossed it out! . . . the *only* word he's written so far – and he's gazing off into space! Ah! . . . Oh dear – he's signed his name again . . . But he's . . . No, he's down again and writing . . . He's written 'the' again – he's crossed it out again, and he's written 'a'. And there's a second word coming up straight away, and it's 'sat'. 'A sat'? Doesn't make sense. 'A Satur'? 'A Saturday'! It's 'A Saturday' . . . And it's 'afternoon'. 'A Saturday afternoon' – it's a confident beginning. And he's straight onto the next word – it's 'in'. 'A Saturday afternoon in . . .' In . . . in . . . in . . . 'No . . .' – November? November's spelt wrong: he's left out the second 'e'. But he's not going back – it looks as though he's going for the *sentence*! . . .'[9]

The scene was supposedly a sports commentary on Thomas Hardy as he began to write *The Return of the Native*, but it is a fairly accurate representation of a common phenomenon in schools. Useful as it may be to some fluent writers to have their pages covered in 'crossings out', as a kind of map of directions they are exploring, children's 'false starts' with pen and paper, and their efforts to obscure them, build steadily up into a major disincentive to write at all. The word-processor can help them get started and keep going. They need not be inhibited by the thought of making mistakes: there's no longer the same kind of 'risk' in committing themselves. As Stephen Marcus has put it, words are no longer carved in stone: they are 'written in light'.[10]

Since it is as easy to make a large change as a small one, children tend to be more keen to experiment and revise their writing using a word-processor. There is also less reason for them to be defensive about criticisms from readers, since it is less of an effort to implement the ones they agree with! Children new to word-processing also tend to write longer texts than they have done previously. In view of these observations it should be no surprise that most people also find that using a word-processor slows them down rather than speeding them up: they tend to indulge in far more 'local editing' than they would normally do, without necessarily making any significant qualitative improvement. One hears tales of teachers having to tell children to stop writing because they have done enough editing for one day: others might envy them their situation.

Some characteristics of the medium

Marshall McLuhan's most famous utterance was that 'the medium is the message'. It is not always easy to be conscious of the ways in which the characteristics of a particular medium are having an effect on its users, independent of the actual messages it is used to communicate. Writing with a word-processor is quite different from writing with a pen or a typewriter: as a writing medium it has special characteristics which make it particularly suitable for some purposes and less suitable for others. Becoming conscious of such effects could help us to use the medium in the ways which seem to suit us best.

One characteristic of writing stored on a word-processor disc is that it is never finished. When one has to write an article in a very short time it may be more prudent to use the typewriter than the word-processor. Using a typewriter, it's easier to say to yourself, 'I could have phrased that sentence a little more elegantly, but it's not worth retyping the whole page: I'll leave it at that.' That's a phenomenon worth knowing about when you have a deadline to meet, but it's also an example of the appropriateness of different writing media for different purposes. Using a word-processor does not mean rejecting the typewriter or the pen, although many of the functions of these latter are, for an increasing number of writers, becoming more efficiently executed with a computer.

Many computer enthusiasts, including some teachers and children, are particularly conscious of the medium as a 'machine' (although the only moving parts are the keys) and have suggested that computers may have a direct effect on the writer's 'creativity'. This may be expressed either as a humanist fear of mechanical intervention in a mystical process, or as a belief that word-processors may liberate the writer from a concern with mechanical chores. One young teenager referred to the fact that the word-processor freed him from his usual writing pattern, in which he spent 'a long time writing and very little time being creative'. In fact research by Colette Daiute at Columbia University so far suggests that 'some young writers work more creatively when they use word processing programs than when they use pens, but the computer makes no difference or is limiting for others'.[11] She divides 'creativity' in writing into 'structural creativity' and 'semantic creativity'. The former includes revision (as well as experimentation with new sentence patterns), and her findings confirm that the use of computers can stimulate such creativity, but observes that 'we have not seen evidence that it affects semantic creativity',[12] by which she refers to the use of words in novel ways, and the presentation of stories or arguments from novel points of view.

Here is a text which was drafted on a word-processor by Janie, an American 11-year-old:

> This may sound pretty weird and sad but sometimes I dream that the whole world would blow up. Another person and I would be the only survivers and we together would start the world all over again. The other person and me would rule the world. We would learn all the technology we need to know,how to fly and airplanes, and all that stuff. We would also learn to care for eachother.I think I would rule the world better than the president rules the United States of America,I hate to say it but its what I think.

On reading this over, Janie declared that she thought 'it was fine'. But here is her revision of the same text on the word-processor:

> This may sound weird but I dream that the whole world would blow up.Another person and I would be the only survivors.We would start the world all over again. We would rule the world together. We would also care for eachother a great deal. We would learn the technology we need to know, how to fly airplanes, and all that stuff. I think I would rule the world better than president Regan rules the United States. I hate to say it but its what I feel.[13]

The differences may appear to be minimal. In fact the passage involved far more revision than Janie had been used to before using the computer. Paragraphing has been introduced, words have been deleted and others added, a spelling has been corrected, sentences have been shuffled around, details have been added.

Colette Daiute suggests that it represents a more 'objective' view of the text. Janie's comment that the first draft was fine suggests that she was obliged to produce a further version. If this is so a loss of spontaneity was perhaps inevitable. But we should perhaps ask ourselves whether the formality of the medium may play a part in this. The text has been condensed: a hundred words have become eighty-eight, and the sentences are less extended. 'We would also learn to care for eachother' is replaced with 'We would also care for eachother a great deal'. Perhaps there is less of a gentle touch, but is there a loss of feeling? The replacement of 'its what I think' with 'its what I feel' suggests not. But we should surely be wary of the danger that a word-processor may make it easier for a child to assuage the anxieties of adults about the mechanics of presentation at the cost of losing something of deeper value to the writer.

One might argue (perhaps simply with a bias absorbed from print) that with a restricted window on your text you may find it difficult to grasp the overall shape of your writing. I still find this a problem when I write with the word-processor, but a teenage student declared that it had the opposite effect on him: he finds that this constraint forces him to plan more carefully because he always has to ask himself 'How does this fit into my overall plan?'. Whether making a virtue of necessity in this way is likely to become characteristic of young users of the new medium is difficult to predict. I have met 7-year-olds in Newcastle who have been using a British hand-held word-processor called the Microwriter with a calculator-style display screen on which they might see only a few words at a time. They were puzzled by my concern about seeing their whole text, and seemed quite happy with being able to 'scroll' the text backwards and forwards, viewing tiny chunks at a time. When I asked if they used the facility for plugging the device into a conventional television screen so that they could see at least a larger section of their text I was told that they did this infrequently. Perhaps they will simply develop approaches to writing which are different from, rather than weaker than, those adopted by writers whose perspectives have been shaped by the pen and the typewriter.

As well as showing that current word-processing systems can make it difficult for some writers to keep in sight the overall shape and content of their text, I have already alluded to a tendency for such systems to lead to an excessive preoccupation with minor details. Allan Collins of Bolt Beranek and Newman refers to such phenomena as 'downsliding' – concentrating on lower and lower

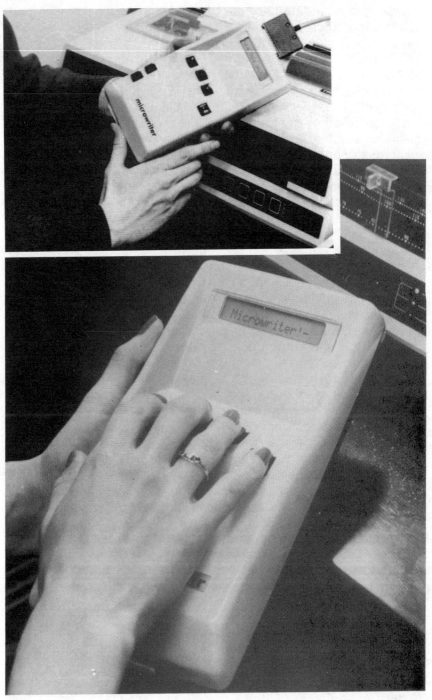

The Microwriter: a British hand-held word processor.

structural levels of text. A programmer friend of mine, Stephen Butler, speculates that 'Perhaps the reading of text from a screen is different from reading a book in that one tends to concentrate on the surface features of syntax and exact meaning at the expense of back-of-consciousness stylistic, subtextual pickups and connections that one makes [when] reading a book and this will influence the type of writing done'.[14] Or perhaps the development of new kinds of word-processors such as those which offer 'multiple windows' on text and others which offer options for various kinds of structural analysis will change all this.

Seeing yourself as a writer

More radically, perhaps, using a word-processor can have effects on the way in which children see themselves as writers. Children writing with word-processors tend to have a greater pride in their writing since they can make it look how they would like it to look. This does not mean that they will necessarily be unrealistic about the actual quality of their writing: one 10-year-old astutely observed that 'the computer makes my writing look better than it is'! However, at least with a good quality printer, the gap which a child perceives between her writing and that which she reads on a professionally printed page is eliminated. The psychological barrier is broken, so that children can come to see themselves as writers.

Dr Mike Sharples of the Department of Artificial Intelligence at Edinburgh University comments on his use of a word-processor with two 11-year-olds in Scotland: 'They were both poor writers with atrocious handwriting, and saw writing as an imposed chore. They used a word-processor to compose articles for the local newspaper. I emphasized the layout – using a good quality printer, right-justifying the text, etc., and they began to see that the gap between their writing and the letters/articles printed in the paper had closed. They sent off the articles and they were published. That alone gave them an enormous boost of confidence, but I doubt that they would even have attempted to write the articles had they not been able to use the printer and formatter.'[15]

As well as providing the boost of simply having access to a tool which many professional writers now use, a word-processor is a supportive medium for children to engage in extended writing, the only way in which they will ever become writers (although access alone cannot be expected to provide a sense of *purpose*). Whenever you write you are also *reading* your words, of course, but it seems that through using a word-processor you are more likely to acquire the habit of re-reading with a critical eye, or in Frank Smith's words, 'reading as a writer'. Furthermore, as Alvin Toffler discovered when considering the effect of reading his words on the video-screen, you come 'closer to seeing them as a *reader* [my emphasis] while still working as a writer'.[16] Young children have considerable difficulty in standing back from their writing and seeing it as someone else might read it. Whether using a word-processor will indeed make this easier for children remains to be demonstrated. Certainly, the earlier you realize that you are writing at least partly for other people the stronger will be your motivation to write: what a delight it can be for a child of 7 to hear that a 5-year-old has enjoyed reading a story she has written for younger children. You are more likely to be conscious of an audience if you know that you will easily be able to produce copies which you can give to people to read and comment on. And, despite the increasing importance of the screen as a reading medium, it is still easier to see yourself as an author when you see your words in print.

Collaborative writing

One frequently unnoticed characteristic of the conventional word-processor is that it is a public medium. At least until a flat, full-page LCD display becomes an alternative to the video-screen, electronic text is on display, not flat on a desk: it is writing which is made to be shared. What are disadvantages in some applications become advantages in others, of course. It is not a very suitable medium for personal writing, for instance, unless you shut yourself away in a room on your own. From the point of view of children's writing, however, a major advantage is that the process of writing can, when desired, be shared with others: it is physically much easier to do this using a keyboard than with pens. The word-processor makes the process far closer to being simultaneous than in a conventional exchange of co-authored material. The use of several Microwriters attached to a BBC Microcomputer is ideal for this purpose, but even with a conventional keyboard one may see three hands on the keys at once.

Genuinely collaborative writing (particularly with an adult) is of considerable value to the young learner. In such a situation, as Frank Smith has pointed out, no-one can say who wrote the text: 'It's rather like carrying a table – you can't say 'I carried it, but he helped''.[17] If writing as a collaborative act becomes widespread as an early introduction to the written word this could begin to erode the traditional concept of authorship.

Collaborative writing is a powerful way to introduce young children to reading and writing at the same time. There is nothing particularly new about this concept: enlightened adults have been using it with children for some years. But the ease with which the activity can be undertaken on a word-processor may simply mean that it happens where it might not have done before, and the immediacy which this tool makes possible can result in the activity becoming more interesting than it would have been without. With an adult or older child acting as keyboard operator, a young child or group of children can decide what they would like to write, and watch their own words appearing on the screen. Changes suggested in what has been written can be easily incorporated (which is difficult if not impossible using other media), and copies of the finished product can be printed so each child has her own copy. Virginia Bradley reports on the use of this technique with small groups of children aged between 6 and 7:

> Children seemed to be highly motivated by seeing their spoken language appear on the screen and were eager to contribute ideas and to read the sentences as they were displayed . . . Aside from the novelty of using the microcomputer a significant factor in the children's enjoyment . . . seemed to be the speed at which their dictation could be transcribed. Writing sentences on a wall chart takes so much time that the children often get restless and bored before the story is finished . . . Once children realized how easily changes could be made, they suggested revisions voluntarily and freely . . . Getting the printed copy of the story immediately stimulated great excitement and unprompted rereading by all of the children . . .[18]

Groups of children can use a word-processing system to create their own books, which other children are often more keen to read than adult products of the printing press. Where they have access to professional-quality printers, this will surely result in children feeling far less remote from published text.

Thus the computer provides us with a powerful technological means to abolish the traditional distinction between writers as producers and readers as consumers. If the fate of the typewriter and photocopier in schools is anything to go by, it seems unlikely that such a revolution will be initiated there. However, in society at large computer networks and 'electronic mail' are changing the character of communication, eroding the notion of one-way output from an author, enabling more people to have the experience of producing their own texts, and allowing them to share them with a larger (ultimately global) readership. Mike Sharples has suggested that 'this, more than any other aspect of computing is going to alter children's perception of the written word'.[19]

Writing aids

A child does not turn into a writer when she is given a dictionary, a thesaurus and a style manual. Children learn about the conventions of writing largely through reading, but not through reading about writing. Once one feels comfortable with writing, reference sources may sometimes be useful, although to many young writers a more efficient means of checking their spelling and punctuation might seem more valuable, given the importance which schools and society accord to clerical accuracy.

Such aids can be incorporated into sophisticated word-processing systems, although my own feeling is that this is a secondary advantage of the medium for writers. A system called WALTER, developed by Mike Sharples in Scotland, incorporates a thesaurus which the child herself can extend. On summoning the function, she would be prompted with 'Word to be looked up?' and might respond with 'big', for which she would then be provided with all the associated words she had previously chosen to list under that heading, such as large, huge, gigantic and so on. The same system even includes options which allow the writer to perform such grammatical transformations of her text as combining short sentences into longer ones using relative clauses. The writer might, for instance, initially enter a text such as this:

> Once there was a pretty princess. The princess lived in a big castle in a forest. The forest was dark. She was very lonely because she had no friends to play with.

On choosing the combining option, the text would be transformed:

> Once there was a pretty princess who lived in a big castle in a dark forest. She was very lonely because she had no friends to play with.[20]

In the United States, Bell Laboratories have created a system called WRITER'S WORKBENCH which offers the writer the option not only of having her spelling checked against an in-built (but extendable) wordbank, but also of having the program offer advice on the punctuation and style. Such options will inevitably become more widely available in word-processing systems suitable for children. The educational implications of this remain to be explored.

The destruction of literacy

Although, as I have suggested, the word-processor, like any other medium, may support and extend some strategies (as well as frustrating others) technology is not central to the process of writing, whether we are talking of the pen, the typewriter or the computer. It is the content of the writing which should always be accorded more importance than the medium. The widely praised capability of the computer to 'motivate' young children to write is hollow indeed if the writer has no genuine purpose in doing so. The computer may be used in schools (as in offices) to lull the users into accepting more submissively a meaningless and oppressive ritual just as easily as it may be used with sensitivity to meet genuine personal needs.

The dangerous myth of the 'neutrality' of technology (in the broadest sense) may indeed blind us to realizing that there is always a built-in bias. It is easier to produce software which reduces 'learning' to a mechanical activity than it is to produce a tool which meets genuine needs. Using computers to drill children in the mechanical 'skills' of spelling, punctuation and 'grammar' will not make them into writers: it will destroy the vitality of their writing and may also destroy their desire to write. Robotic exercises in 'word attack', 'vocabulary building', 'comprehension' will not make children into competent readers: they will make reading seem a lifeless process and may therefore destroy their desire to read. And yet, as I demonstrated in chapter 1, not only do current commercial programs seem to be little other than electronic drill, but the tendency is for the bulk of such software to concentrate on the kinds of exercises which are easiest to computerize, with the result that most of the available software represents an inversion of educational priorities rather than a reflection of children's needs.

For instance, of 253 programs specifically for 'reading development' in thirty-two US software catalogues in 1982, fifty-six per cent dealt with word attack, thirty-seven per cent with comprehension and six per cent with 'study skills'.[21] A subdivision of the first two categories provides a vivid illustration of the inversion of priorities:

Word Attack

Phonics	50%
Dictionary skills	20%
Structural analysis	20%
Context analysis	5%
Sight words	4%

Comprehension

Vocabulary building	72%
Literal comprehension	20%
Interpretative comprehension	8%

As computers continue to become cheaper, and 'network systems' of linked microcomputers spread in the schools, it looks likely that they will be used to provide 'individualized' instruction in increasingly narrow 'skills' rather than being used as liberating tools such as word-processors. It is in this sense, as Frank Smith recently declared, that 'computers could destroy literacy.'[22] My purpose here has been simply to expose some of the issues so that a more conscious decision may be taken to positively discriminate in favour of the use of computers in ways which genuinely extend young children's capabilities in writing and reading. Whether we shall take such a direction depends on us: technology won't take us there.

4

Getting wise to 'information'

JUDGE: I have read your case, Mr Smith, and I am no wiser now than I was when I started.
SMITH: Possibly not, My Lord, but far better informed.[1]

Children are not computers. They do not passively absorb data from the world and 'process' it: they *create* the world in their own minds, turning into information only that which relates to their understanding of what things are like. The potency of the computer metaphor is such that its early use in cognitive psychology has been widely abused: learning is now loosely described as 'information processing' by those who then imply that it consists of no more than the mechanical processing of data. Whilst this may be an accurate description of the bulk of the activities which still take place in institutionalized education, it is an impoverished vision of the human brain. Let me make one of my underlying assumptions clear: information is the least important factor in thinking and learning.

Ironically, consciousness of the educational limitations of 'transmitting' facts is being heightened by the spread of electronic 'information retrieval' systems. One powerful message of such systems is that facts are constantly changing. This will tend to reinforce a realization that there is little value in attempting to teach children facts in the belief that they will be useful to them throughout their lives. As the availability of cheap calculators has undermined the purpose of rote-learning tables, so the increasing accessibility of databases challenges the purpose of the rote-learning of facts. However, the time it is taking for the pocket calculator to achieve such a revolution in attitudes in schools does not encourage one to be particularly optimistic about the short-term effect of the routine use of computer databases.

One response from educational institutions in Britain to the ever-increasing threat to the place of facts in education has been to add something called 'information skills' to the curriculum, the essence of which is regarded as being an ability to 'handle' facts. The phrase itself has disturbing overtones: the reference to 'skills' rather than strategies, and the implied focus on 'information' rather than learning. With the publication of this book in 1984 one might also be tempted to muse on the Orwellian possibilities of making access to information conditional upon being given instruction in how to use it. As an institutional reform it certainly shifts the focus of learning from 'What?' to 'How?', but it still ignores the question 'Why?' As I have written elsewhere, to attempt to teach 'information skills' in the context of an 'information'-centred curriculum will only produce users of 'information' with increasingly less use for it.[2] This is not to deny the usefulness of knowing how to find something out, of course, but only to suggest that such know-how loses much of its value in otherwise unchanged educational institutions. Where a child's learning really is self-directed – where she has decided for herself that there is something she wishes to find out – the same know-how can be liberating, particularly bearing in mind the new possibilities which computer-based systems can offer to the user.

Isaac Asimov once said that 'man should be ashamed to do things that machines can do better'. The brain is very inefficient at deliberately assimilating large quantities of data, human memory is too creative to act like a database, and our efforts at 'number crunching' are pitifully slow and inaccurate by comparison with a calculator. There are far better uses for the human brain.

Using computers as a medium for the storage, retrieval and sorting of large quantities of data presents itself as an appropriate use of the technology, leaving the creators to select material appropriate for such storage, and users to interpret it (and to bear in mind its limitations). At present, publicly-available 'viewdata' systems such as Prestel in Britain, Telidon in Canada and The Source in the US allow users to call up 'frames' on their television receivers from a mainframe computer by using the telephone system. The main function of such databases is as a 'public information service'. Typically, several hundred frames offer up-to-date news and weather bulletins, sports results, travel information, and regional entertainment guides, and many thousands of frames offer general and specialized business statistics, since the system is largely paid for by business-users. Concessions to children may well be made ('kidstuff' frames and 'interactive' games are common) but most of their routine reference needs are not catered for by such systems at present. And in any case, children have limited access to them. The range of these databases is commonly thought of as encyclopaedic but is in fact far from being so. Even on some of the topics which they do cover viewdata systems cannot compare in depth of coverage with alternative sources of reference. The London magazine *Time Out*, for instance, provides a cheap list of all the entertainment events currently running in the city in around 100 pages, which would take thousands of Prestel's 200,000 or so frames and therefore be uneconomic in a viewdata system.

To transfer the contents of every book in the British Library or the Library of Congress to conventional computer storage would require a computer with a memory capacity approximately a thousand times larger than any in existence at present, and a telephone network of far greater transmission capacity to make it possible to read (especially if the books include photographs) at a reasonable rate.[3] Video-discs, fibre-optics, cable TV and satellites could begin to solve some of the problems of capacity, but more importantly, it will surely take many more years for an electronic medium to incorporate all the advantages of books. Therefore, in the medium term at least, moves towards an encyclopaedia rather than a library are the best we can expect.

When such systems do metamorphose into something worthy of being described as an 'Encyclopaedia Galactica', they are thus likely to be only one kind of reference source: providing a new kind of popular reference source on a scale previously unknown in the home. They are unlikely to become a substitute for specialized books. Scientists using the medium have reported difficulty in studying material on the video screen, and although print-out facilities could be used, this would hardly be practicable for entire books. Rather than replacing books as a primary reading medium, it seems likely that ways of exploiting their particular strengths will continue to be developed.

One well-established use of the medium is in providing pointers to 'where to look things up'. Isaac Asimov writes that 'the sum total of human knowledge lacks an index, and . . . there is no efficient method of retrieval of information. How can we correct this but by calling on a more-than-human memory to serve as an index, and a faster-than-human system of retrieval to make use of the index?'.[4] Computer-based bibliographic retrieval systems are already widely used in libraries. They act as sophisticated subject-indexes, allowing users to find out the titles of books and articles on particular topics by asking them to specify a number of keywords which describe the precise topic they are interested in. Such systems are becoming increasingly heavily used , but currently most are not geared to the needs of young children. The extension of such a system, allowing all users to request copies of the books from their homes, which is a facility which could be incorporated into a viewdata system, would

have considerable benefits, but is not likely to be implemented in
the short-term. The priority, once more, is the establishment of
shopping and banking facilities.

The most un-booklike potential use for databases is in association
with what are known as 'expert systems'. Such software is designed
to try to answer certain simple questions on a specific subject, such
as car repair or botanical identification. When they are created by
specialists in the field for the use of non-specialists, expert systems
are clearly likely to be useful in certain limited and well-defined
areas of human knowledge. They could be educative to use and
even more educative to create or at least expand and personalize.
Children would enjoy creating their own simple 'expert systems' on
their areas of expertise – their hobbies, since they would in effect
be 'teaching' the machines. Primitive tools for them to do so are
beginning to become available, although the artificial intelligentsia
would not consider them worthy of the title of expert systems, which
they reserve for grander systems incorporating an element of
learning from 'experience' as well as from instruction, and,
operating on probabilities, that emulate the judgement of human
'experts' when meeting previously unencountered problems.

Software is easily available for a modest use of microcomputer-
based databases as methods of storing and retrieving data for
personal use. Indeed, it is perhaps this application for databases
which is of most obvious immediate utility to children. Awareness
and use of regional, national or even international retrieval systems
is only part of what some refer to as 'information literacy'. However,
guided tours of someone else's frame of reference are not enough.
Children are seldom allowed to contribute to such databases, still
less accorded equal priority. If we do not want them to grow up as
the alienated consumers of chickfeed provided by the information-
rich then we must give them tools with which to create their own
systems for sharing information with each other. And if we are to
ensure that self-generated databases are to become serious
educational aids then we must surely make them available from the
earliest possible age.

FACTFILE (Cambridge University Press, 1982) is a simple program
which which was designed as a result of a seminar at the University
of Cambridge Department of Education in 1981.[5] Teachers and
children in primary schools, it was felt, needed a gentle introduction
to the storage and retrieval of data on a microcomputer which did
not require the coded commands of the sophisticated information-
retrieval systems. The program may serve to illustrate at least the
most elementary functions of computer database systems for those
who may not be familiar with them.

The program allows users to build up their own files of data on any topic which they choose. The first two frames look like this:

```
        Welcome
          to
        FACTFILE

      Press RETURN
```

[User presses RETURN key]

```
        Choice Page
      You can
      A make a file
      B change a file
      C look at a file
      D start again

      Press A, B, C or D
```

Let us suppose that a group of children decide to create a file on British trees. They press A and the screen changes:

```
        Make a file

    What is your file called?

    Type it then press RETURN
```

They type 'TREES' and press RETURN. A few frames later they are prompted with this:

```
        Make a file

    How many headings do you have
    for each TREE?

    Type it then press RETURN
```

Now they need to think carefully about what kind of material they would like to include in the file. This will depend partly on what they already know about trees and partly on what they think other people will find it useful to know about. They may start off by deciding that they would like to include the maximum height, and the colour and type of the leaves and bark. This may take some time. But eventually they may decide that they will have five headings.

```
┌─────────────────────────────────────┐
│                                     │
│            Make a file              │
│                                     │
│       What is the 1st heading?      │
│                                     │
│     Type it then press RETURN       │
│                                     │
└─────────────────────────────────────┘
```

They type HEIGHT, and are prompted to supply the other five headings. Then the screen changes again:

```
┌─────────────────────────────────────┐
│                                     │
│            Make a file              │
│                                     │
│     What is the 1st TREE called?    │
│                                     │
│     Type it then press RETURN       │
│                                     │
└─────────────────────────────────────┘
```

They might agree to start with the yew.

```
┌─────────────────────────────────────┐
│                                     │
│            Make a file              │
│                                     │
│   What is the HEIGHT entry for the  │
│   YEW?                              │
│                                     │
│     Type it then press RETURN       │
│                                     │
└─────────────────────────────────────┘
```

It is quite unlikely that they will have any idea to what maximum height the yew has been known to grow, so they consult some reference books. When they eventually track down a reference to such a statistic they then need to decide what unit of measurement to use. They may choose metres.

```
┌─────────────────────────────────────────┐
│             Make a file                   │
│                                           │
│   What is the LEAF-TYPE entry for the     │
│                 YEW?                      │
│                                           │
│       Type it then press RETURN           │
└─────────────────────────────────────────┘
```

This may cause a little discussion, and a great deal more consultation of reference books, but they may eventually decide on a series of labels to refer to types of leaf. In this case it might be NEEDLES. When it comes to 'bark type' they finally decide that their reference books have very limited illustrations, so they postpone any further additions to the file until they have done a survey of local trees.

And so it goes on, until eventually they have a file of data on perhaps sixty trees stored on their microcomputer. They may well have totally rethought their original headings, adding genus and species, and keys to whether they are native, deciduous or evergreen. By now they may be quite proud of its advantages over some of the reference books they have used: they may have offset the system's lack of illustrations by developing an accompanying booklet for users to refer to. Now they are ready to allow some other children to try it out.

```
┌─────────────────────────────────────────┐
│             Look at a file                │
│                                           │
│   You can                                 │
│   A see all the TREES                     │
│   B see one TREE                          │
│   C ask something else                    │
│   D go back to the Choice Page            │
│                                           │
│          Press A, B, C or D               │
└─────────────────────────────────────────┘
```

The users might decide to find out which are the native evergreen trees. Initially they would need to be told that the way to find this out is by pressing C.

```
┌─────────────────────────────────────┐
│          Look at a file             │
│                                     │
│   How many headings do you want     │
│          to look at?                │
│                                     │
│    Type it then press RETURN        │
└─────────────────────────────────────┘
```

They type 2 and the screen changes again.

```
┌─────────────────────────────────────┐
│          Look at a file             │
│                                     │
│     What is the 1st heading?        │
│                                     │
│    Type it then press RETURN        │
└─────────────────────────────────────┘
```

They are told to enter the code 'DECID OR E/G' and they go through the same process again with the code 'NATIVE'. Eventually they reach this frame:

```
┌─────────────────────────────────────┐
│          Look at a file             │
│                                     │
│   You want to see all the TREES     │
│   with                              │
│   DECID OR E/G: E/G                  │
│   NATIVE: YES                        │
│   Is that correct?                  │
│                                     │
│       Type YES or NO                │
└─────────────────────────────────────┘
```

They agree, and in a few seconds the screen lists all those trees which the original group had listed as both native and evergreen, in alphabetical order.

No reference book can do this, and although this particular program is rather plodding and primitive in concept, I hope it will have provided at least a taste of the *use* to which children can put such systems. Equally important is the child's developing sense of the limitations of a database. A simple example may help to bring this out. During the testing of FACTFILE one group of 8-year-olds in Cambridgeshire was asked to make a very simple file on the weather based on a diary with which they were provided. Emma's diary dealt with one week in winter, mentioning sunshine, rain, wind and snow, so the group used these as headings, and recorded 'yes' or 'no' for each day. The diary was then taken away, and the group was asked a series of questions.

They began innocently enough with questions such as 'What was the weather like on Tuesday?' for which the 'see one DAY' option was selected. With a question such as 'On which days did it snow?' they simply requested the days when they had entered YES under the SNOW heading. But they began to discover how difficult it could be to decide which headings to search when they were asked such questions as 'Which was the best day to build a snowman?'. They were becoming conscious of the importance of being clear about which questions are being asked. When asked 'On what days did Emma need to wear wellingtons to walk to school?', they requested the rainy days, and offered the answer of Sunday as well as Friday, forgetting that she would not have been at school on Sunday. In this case they were learning that the inadequacy of the original structure may mean that you need to do some sifting afterwards yourself. This was not what adults might quickly have described as 'computer error'.

Young children can use microcomputer-based databases as powerful aids to self-directed learning in a wide variety of applications, such as opinion-polls, studies of the weather, traffic surveys, pollution measures and the observation of the distribution of plants and animals.

A good example of an approach to data-processing which arose from children's real interests rather than being imposed on them is a project undertaken at Fox Primary school in London. It concerns conkers. Readers outside Britain may not know that conkers are hard, brown, nut-like seeds found inside the spiky green husks from the horse-chestnut tree, or that 'conkers' is a contest with conkers on strings to determine which of the seeds can survive the most buffeting. In autumn 1982 some of the children (mostly aged 9) had been discussing what made a good conker. Folklore recipes were recounted in which conkers were soaked in vinegar or slowly baked to make them harder. The skin thickness, weight and size of a conker were all discussed as factors which might contribute to its strength. Some felt that older conkers tended to be best, others preferred heavy ones, and others felt that conkers should be either very small or very large to fare well in a tournament. Their teacher, Dr Alistair Ross, was intrigued by the scientific dimension of this debate and challenged them to find out the characteristics of 'the strongest conker in the world'.

They measured the weight and volume of 209 conkers, and after some debate agreed on a method of measuring a conker's strength by dropping a standard weight on each one from increasing heights until a crack appeared. Skin thickness was then measured with a micrometer screw gauge, averages being taken from readings taken in three positions. A note was also made of the time which had elapsed since the collection of each conker from under the horse-chestnut trees. All the measurements were entered on a chart. The problem was that the chart was about 5 metres long, so that by simply looking at the data it was difficult to detect any patterns.

This was an ideal opportunity to use a data-handling program on their microcomputer (they used a program called micro-LEEP). They gave each conker a number, and entered the date when it was found, its weight in grams, its volume in cubic centimetres, its strength (in terms of the height in centimetres at which a one kilogram weight cracked it), its age in days since collection, the thickness of the skin in millimetres, and so on. When all the data had been entered the testing of hypotheses was much easier. The computer could search rapidly through all the data for records of conkers which matched any criteria which the children had specified. For instance, asking for all the two-day-old conkers involved specifying 'AGE=2'; and 'AGE<4 AND STRENGTH>30' was the formula for getting the computer to list all the conkers which were less than four days old and which had not cracked until the weight had been dropped from more than 30 centimetres. The children were then able to ask to have printed out only the particular data in which they were specially interested, in the order in which they wanted to see it. The computer could also print out histograms and graphs of the distribution of weights, strengths and volumes for conkers which the children categorized as 'large', 'medium' and 'small' (after they had decided exactly what they meant by these terms). Looking for possible patterns became much easier: the computer allowed the children to concentrate on interpreting the data. The considerable 'mechanical' chore of testing hypotheses manually against such large quantities of data can be a major disincentive to exploring alternative theories (especially for children). Here, the computer offered a supportive medium for doing precisely that, allowing the children to behave like human beings rather than machines.

The results were fascinating scientific discoveries for those children. For instance, older conkers did not seem to be stronger than fresh ones. It was found, in fact, that the strength of a conker declines by almost 50% in the first twelve days from falling from the tree, although it regains a little of its strength over a year. The children who had felt that large and heavy conkers seemed stronger also seemed justified in their claims. Dr Ross reported that the children's reactions to these discoveries were interesting: at the time, they felt that their discoveries should remain a secret so that they might employ them to their own advantage against other conker players in the following season. He commented, 'Clearly, the next lesson must be about the morals of public information of scientific discovery'.[6]

Using a database has not become central to the learning process, of course, but it has some strong advantages in particular applications. Where it is desirable to consider a large quantity of data or a wide range of observations, the use of a database can make it easier for children to make useful generalizations. With easily manipulable data hypotheses can be made and tested on a range of phenomena far broader than those routinely encountered by the individual, and more extensive and formal analysis becomes possible for children. 'Data-processing' is one way of developing a more systematic approach to problem-solving, in which, for instance, planning, categorization, and formal reasoning are demanded. This kind of activity can provide a framework for the articulated exercise and extension of that hypothesis-making which goes on in our brains all the time, and which is the foundation of our most effective learning. The value of the activity as well as the 'validity' of its findings is dramatically extended when it involves the sharing both of ideas and the business of investigation. Indeed it is in the languaging rather than in the use of the computer as such that the real learning takes place: enabling children to talk and write together about something far closer to 'research' than many of the activities which pass under that name in many schools.

5

Learning to control computers

'The question is,' said Humpty Dumpty, 'which is to be master
– that's all.'

Lewis Carroll[1]

Some enthusiastic teachers have described the use of 'Speak and Spell', the hand-held electronic spelling test, as 'enabling children to direct their own learning'. This would seem to mean that they are allowed to press the buttons themselves and need not trouble an adult to tell them whether they have spelled something accurately. This is not the direction of learning: it is the pacing of testing.[2] When using technology, real control of one's learning must involve some degree of control of the technology which is more than simply reactive. Children would learn far more about spelling, about learning and about controlling technology by writing a spelling program and discovering its limitations for themselves.

Programming might be thought of as an attempt to make a computer do what you want it to do in the language it allows you to use. In this sense a 5-year-old who is able to make an electronic toy such as Bigtrak move forward, backward or turn by pressing the arrow and number keys is programming her little truck in the same sense that her 12-year-old brother is doing so when typing into his microcomputer the coded instructions to create his own arcade games. The 12-old has a far greater range of options, but in both cases the locus of control is far closer to the user than if either were using an explicitly 'educational' toy such as 'Speak and Spell', in which they could more accurately be described as being programmed by the machine.

Bigtrak

Bigtrak[3] is an interesting example of a pathway into computer control for young children. It is a toy which has been widely used by children as young as six years old, but seems to be most popular with children of around eight and nine.[4] Microprocessor-based, the plastic vehicle is about a foot long: on the top is a calculator-like keypad which allows the user to select in advance a sequence of movements which the truck then performs. Andrew, an English 9-year-old, describes his own reaction to it: 'When I first saw Bigtrak I thought it was a remote controlled vehicle. One thing I didn't understand was how it worked but I do now. You press some buttons on it and away it goes . . . I found the programming a bit difficult but I liked watching it move across the floor . . . Another thing I didn't understand was how it turned but I do now. 15 means quarter of a turn, 30 means half a turn and 45 means three quarters of a turn and 60 means a full one.' Andrew adds, 'I think Big Trak has helped me improve my mathematics'. Indeed, in learning to control Bigtrak children do develop some important mathematical strategies, such as estimating angle and distance (allowing for the friction of different floor surfaces), but the broader learning includes breaking a problem into a logical sequence of steps and the formulation and testing of hypotheses.

The toy can be programmed to manoeuvre its way around obstacle courses, to flash its lights and emit electronic sounds, to operate a tipper trailer, and, with a number of other such toys, to perform a complex formation dance. Nevertheless, its functions are limited, and, as Zoe, a 13-year-old English girl commented, 'I spent an evening playing with Bigtrak. I realise that perhaps it was not aimed at my age group, but I was a little bored with it by the time I had discovered its limits . . . If aimed at eight year or nine year-olds, quite feasible for a month or two, but I think the obvious limits of the toy would bore the child before long'.

Bigtrak is a special-purpose robot. An uncommitted computer, on the other hand, is as Papert puts it 'the Proteus of machines . . . It can take on a thousand forms and can serve a thousand functions, it can appeal to a thousand tastes'.[5]

Programming a computer

In British primary schools and US elementary schools it is still the case that relatively few children are writing computer programs, and yet almost all of them are probably capable of learning to do so. A major barrier to children learning programming in the schools is still the scarcity of computers. One national survey undertaken in the US by Dr Carl Smith of Indiana University in 1982 showed that only 32.6% of schools had at least one microcomputer (only 23.8% of elementary schools). On this basis an equitable distribution of usage would allow the average access for each schoolchild to be only one minute a day. Projections suggest that it will be 1988 before this rises to 46 minutes.[6] In Britain a far higher proportion of primary schools now have computers. At the time of writing (late November 1983), Department of Industry figures revealed that at least 74% of primary schools in England and Wales already had, or would shortly have, at least one microcomputer system under the government scheme. If we allow for those computers acquired by schools independently of the scheme and calculate on the basis of equitable distribution between schools and across the primary age-range the potential average access for each child would still be no more than about one and a half minutes a day.[7]

Even more significant than the numerical distribution of microcomputers in schools is the pattern of use. I can offer no statistics, but many observers would agree that a widespread pattern in American urban school systems is that in the predominantly working-class inner-city areas the emphasis is on using computers to provide 'reinforcement' in 'basic skills', whilst in the middle-class suburbs computers are mainly used by children learning to program. The pattern would not appear to be so clear-cut in Britain as yet, although the declaration that 'pupils will need to learn to use computers, but not all will need to program them' is depressingly widespread.[8]

The institutionalization of the use of the computer may have an alienating effect on some children who might otherwise enjoy the experience. Why should a child who is already keenly teaching herself to program her home computer submit to someone else's primitive instructional software? If schools take away the liberty of children to make decisions about what to do with computers teachers should not be surprised if the initial interest wanes. Rhea, a 9-year-old Canadian, commented that 'I felt it was much better at the computer when . . . nobody was telling me what to do'. In many schools, the tragedy is that the computer is largely used in applications which are sufficiently limited not to disturb the teachers with its potency.

For many young children programming a microcomputer may initially mean simply typing in printed listings of other people's programs (particularly games), often from popular computer magazines. It is easy to dismiss this activity as worthless, but it inevitably involves more than simply 'copying'. It is rare indeed for either the printed copy or the transcription to be accurate and, after the often mammoth task of typing, the errors have to be located and corrected before the program will run. Most children also like to personalize the program, even if only in a minor way. More extensive adaptations have to be made where the program was not written specifically for the computer the child is using. Curiosity may prompt them to examine the structure of the program. One English 12-year-old, Astrid, when asked how she was learning about programming, observed, 'I looked in the listing to see what sort of things made the computer do that, so I learned something about that'. Arthur Leuhrmann, a pioneer of popular computing, said recently that he thinks that the major factor in learning to program may be learning to *read* programs. Once the structure is at least partially understood, children may begin to make changes more purposefully, extending it so that they begin to feel that it is their own.

One 8-year-old girl's first attempt at programming was to type in a listing of a very short program she had found which simply displayed the nine-times table. The listing (here slightly adapted) was in the programming language called BASIC.

```
10 FOR K=0 TO 12
20 PRINT K*9
30 NEXT K
```

The program, when run, prints this:

```
   0
   9
  18
  27
  36
  45
  54
  63
  72
  81
  90
  99
 108
```

Since she was not used to including 0 in her tables, she looked through the listing to see what controlled its appearance. Seeing the 0 in line 10, she retyped the line as 'FOR K=1 TO 12'. Then she inserted a line which added a delay, so that she could repeat each number before the next appeared on the screen. Next, she decided that she wanted the five-times table, so she looked at the listing again and changed 'K*9' to 'K*5'. When run, this version stopped at 60, but she was still counting ahead, being used to stopping at 100 when she counted in fives. So she replaced 'FOR K = 1 TO 12' with 'FOR K = 1 TO 100' only to discover that this caused the program to stop only when it had reached 500. She tried again, replacing 100 with 40, arguing when asked that '60 from 100 leaves 40'. This time the program printed fives up to 200 before stopping. Eventually she realized that 20 would do the trick. An observer comments: 'This was the first formal attempt at programming made by the girl. Her previous experience was limited solely to playing games on the computer and watching older and more experienced people encoding and debugging programs. All the modifications she made were drawn from memory. Her analysis of and amendments to the logic and arithmetical processes were more remarkable for the fact that she was not previously considered capable of such a level of understanding.'[9]

Thinking strategies

A program cannot be judged 'right' or 'wrong'. Programming turns mathematics and logic into a craft: there are simply degrees of versatility or elegance. Hence the experience has more in common with creative activities in which children engage outside school than with most of those peculiar to institutional education. Nevertheless, in attempting to make a program do what she wants it to a child inevitably discovers flaws or 'bugs' in her thinking (or her typing). Programs rarely work at all when run for the first time, and can defy many attempts to make them run exactly as you had expected them to. Some teachers believe that they should protect children from making mistakes by careful planning. It is a view held by many who believe that learning can best be encouraged through rewards and punishments. But programming can allow children to learn from their mistakes, and to develop, test and rework their theories. With the motivation of controlling the machine and the opportunity to share problems with others, it is less discouraging to learn from one's mistakes experimentally on a computer than in a formal instructional context. In a school context a child's reaction to her own mistakes can be to put them out of her mind. But in programming even the professional expects to have to spend a considerable amount of time in 'debugging'. And to fix the bugs, even the novice has to try to understand what happened.

In learning to program one is also learning to be conscious of one's thinking and learning strategies. One young teenager told me that unless I change my ways I'll never make a programmer, because 'although you can be logical, you're not very systematic'! I thought that was a very perceptive observation about qualities which one needs to acquire in order to be efficient as a programmer. Programming requires one to be able to imagine and express clearly the steps needed to accomplish specific tasks. It is essential to be able to define a problem, to use language with precision, to be able to generate effective approaches (with an awareness of which alternatives might be most appropriate), to plan an overall strategy, to break this down into manageable units, to systematically seek out the weaknesses in one's reasoning, and so on. This kind of thinking does not come 'naturally' to adults at present, since our childhood environment was not as supportive of such a style of thinking as the computer-rich environment is. Young programmers have to discipline themselves to think and express their thinking precisely in order to make the computer do what they want it to do. And they can really enjoy thinking like this. Angela, a 10-year-old Canadian, enjoyed using her own skill to create a program: 'You really have to think about what you are doing . . . I like to use my head to figure out the tough questions'. The computer provides a reason to think about and talk about thinking.

In her powerful book, *Children's Minds*, Margaret Donaldson argues that at least as far as institutional education is concerned, to be a successful learner one needs to be sufficiently self-aware to examine and control one's thinking. My own feeling is that such an ability would be a powerful aid to abstract thought even if schools did not exist.

> The normal child comes to school with well-established skills as a thinker. But his thinking is *directed outwards* [her emphasis] to the real, meaningful, shifting, distracting world. What is going to be required for success in our educational system is that he should learn to turn language and thought in upon themselves. He must be able to direct his own thought processes in a thoughtful manner. He must be able not just to talk but to choose what he will say, not just to interpret but to weigh possible interpretations. His conceptual system must expand in the direction of increasing ability to represent itself. He must become capable of manipulating systems.[10]

A fluency in the style of thinking involved in programming may lead children to adopt similar strategies in other contexts. Although there is no conclusive evidence about the 'problem of transfer', Wallace Feurzeig and others have suggested that 'if the transfer is not spontaneous, it probably could be facilitated if adequate attention were given to that goal'.[11] If the strategies do indeed transfer, perhaps the greatest benefit of the computer to a thinker would be to make her more conscious of a range of thinking styles which she was free to select on the basis of suitability for particular purposes. Whether growing up in a computer-rich environment will indeed cause children to become flexible thinkers or whether it will lead to an overvaluing and overuse of rigid rationalism we surely cannot predict, but we should not allow our deprivation of experience of the style of thinking involved in programming to blind us to its possibilities.

Logo: a language for learning

The most widespread programming language (and one which is 'built into' most common microcomputers) is misleadingly called BASIC (Beginners' All-purpose Symbolic Instruction Code). It is in many ways an awkward and untidy language. Even using only a limited subset of the language, 'sufficient for constructing guessing games and simple low resolution graphics', an Oxfordshire primary teacher found that only 20% of his class of children aged between ten and eleven years were able to cope with programming in the language. This dropped to nearer 5% when 'loops' (a repeat function) were introduced. He found that the nature of the language made it difficult to break a programming task into small routines and debugging was a major cause of frustration. The process of coding was not supporting, but 'interposing . . . between the child and its view of the problem'.[12]

Logo, on the other hand, is a computer programming language which was developed specifically for children by Seymour Papert and Wallace Feurzeig at the Massachusetts Institute of Technology in the late 1960s. The educational philosophy which partly led to its development (but which has also blossomed from its use) is described in the best-seller of educational computing, Papert's *Mindstorms*, published in 1980. As an exposition of the Logo language *Mindstorms* does at times seem to ascribe to it power which might reasonably be attributed to the activity of programming *per se*, but many studies have shown that it certainly does possess characteristics which make it particularly appropriate for young learners, and the book itself is an inspirational vision of children's capabilities and the part that computers can play in extending them.

The most striking feature of Logo, for those who don't know it, is its use of graphics. Most users use only the screen-based version, in which simple commands such as 'FORWARD' typed on the standard computer keyboard make the 'screen-turtle' trace a pattern. Luckier learners also have the 'floor-turtle', a special-purpose robot linked to the computer by a cable, which can be made to move along the

A floor turtle in use at St. Cleer's Junior and Infant School,
Liskeard, Cornwall
Photographer: Roger Moss

floor and leave marks on paper in the same manner. Children, of course, greatly enjoy playing with patterns, and this would seem an excellent way of introducing them to the control of computers. Drawing patterns on a screen using the common programming language, BASIC, is a very cumbersome programming task, suited only to those who already have a good grasp of the language. One 11-year-old American boy who had not heard of Logo told me, 'I'm trying to learn graphics but I don't understand all the POKES and PEEKS involved'.

Using Logo children as young as eight can produce sophisticated graphics with the use of simple words. Instead of the rather daunting task of 'learning programming', the child tends to regard what she is doing as discovering how to draw in a different medium, an unusual medium in which you have to specify in words exactly how you want your pencil to behave. Turtle graphics is not just an electronic sketchpad: the user must articulate her intentions for her designs to be realized. 'You have to tell it what's in your mind to get it to do things', observed a child in an English junior school. The user must be explicit about how far forward she wants the turtle to go, or how far she wants it to turn to the right, even if she changes her mind afterwards and tries again.

The description of processes which Logo requires focuses their attention on *how* things work. As Richard Noss has commented, 'the writing and modifying of concise procedures and programs allows for exploration not only of the result, but also of the *means* [my emphasis] by which the result is achieved. It is this which distinguishes the kind of concrete modelling activity possible with Logo, from other thinking tools such as Diene's Logiblocks or Cuisenaire rods'.[13]

The formal language of mathematics thus acquires an obvious purpose for children. A child who doesn't yet know that to achieve a right angle involves rotation by 90 degrees may discover for herself the concept of degrees when she has to tell the computer by how many units she wants the turtle to turn to the right. Beryl Maxwell, a teacher in an English junior school, recalls how one child using Logo exclaimed with delight 'We've discovered a magic number!' when her small group of friends succeeded in making their floor-turtle draw a neat corner. More importantly, once a child has discovered how to create, say, a square, she can 'teach' the computer to remember how it was done simply by giving the operation a name, such as 'SQUARE'. And once she has discovered how to make the turtle make an ARC, she can use two ARCs to make a PETAL, several PETALs to make a FLOWER and many FLOWERs to make a GARDEN.

Logo can provide a supportive environment for a variety of

thinking strategies. Many children find a 'top-down' strategy most effective, breaking their goal into smaller parts. In order to draw a house, a child might break the problem down into drawing a triangle for a roof, drawing a square for the walls, and then combining them. Initially the screen-turtle would be in the middle of the screen, pointing upwards. She could create a square like this:

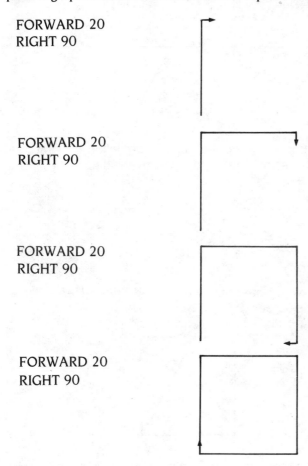

FORWARD 20
RIGHT 90

FORWARD 20
RIGHT 90

FORWARD 20
RIGHT 90

FORWARD 20
RIGHT 90

She might create a roof-shape like this:

RIGHT 90
FORWARD 20
LEFT 120

FORWARD 20
LEFT 120

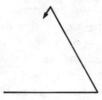

FORWARD 20
LEFT 120

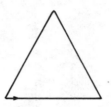

Satisfied with these procedures, she might then define the first as a
BOX and the second as a ROOF. Next she might decide to define
HOUSE something like this:

```
TO HOUSE
BOX
ROOF
END
```

Unfortunately this would have an unexpected effect. Here's what
would appear on the screen:

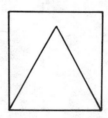

What she would have forgotten is the point at which the turtle would
come to rest at the end of the BOX (the bottom left corner in fact –
exactly where it started). The ROOF procedure would therefore
begin at 'ground level'. She might solve this problem by inserting a
new instruction in the HOUSE procedure, so that after drawing the
BOX, the turtle would move FORWARD 20 again before drawing the
ROOF. Or she might redefine HOUSE so that the ROOF would be
drawn first, since her procedure leaves the turtle pointing to the
right. These (and many more alternative solutions) would produce
this:

The child in this case might not have experienced this problem if she had done what Papert calls 'playing turtle'. This involves acting out the sequence using one's own movements (e.g. walking around the room) to create the desired pattern in space. Papert argues that some kinds of mathematics come very easily to children, for example the mathematics of space and movement, and that turtle-geometry allows children to draw on their mathematical strengths. Children spontaneously relate the movement of the turtle, particularly the floor-turtle, to their own movement in space, and as one observer noted, 'the movements of children's hands, as they indicate to their fellows what is needed, are most impressive. When discussing rotations and displacement they display a degree of involvement which is hard to develop at this age by other methods'.[14]

We have already referred to the usefulness of the concept of 'debugging' one's thinking. Since it is easier to keep the structure of a program clear using Logo than it is using BASIC, 'following the program' does not involve unravelling the spaghetti created by 'GOTO' instructions constantly redirecting the reader. An additional dimension may be that if a child writes a simple Logo program for the turtle to draw a HOUSE and instead produces a square with a triangle inside it her reaction is to see the turtle rather than herself as doing 'the wrong thing'. Consequently it is easy for the child to be objective about the problem, to consider exactly why and where the procedure went wrong.

Logo is therefore both simple to learn *and* powerful as a programming language. One source of its power is the ease with which the child can add to the language itself, introducing her own commands (such as to 'HOUSE'). Users might almost be seen as *creating* their own programming language when they add new procedures to the Logo vocabulary. This in particular sets it apart from most other programming languages commonly available on microcomputers.

The power and accessibility of Logo offer children the opportunity to explore mathematical concepts in a more personal, playful and experimental manner which is less deliberate and structured than in formal instruction. Because this is closer to the way the brain learns most easily it is not surprising that many children given the chance to learn mathematics in this way enjoy the experience, a phenomenon rare in school mathematics. Learning mathematics through using Logo is also not simply 'learning mathematics', it is teaching the machine. (One might argue that only when schools react to the challenge by attempting to graft Logo onto a mathematics curriculum and devising 'worksheets' to ensure that children 'cover' the syllabus is the heart of its appeal to children threatened.) Using computers, children have access to what Papert refers to as a 'mathematics-speaking being', enabling them to explore fundamental concepts in mathematics in an everyday context. Algebra acquires a clear purpose: variables have to be used in programs to handle data which is yet to be entered. Programs are far easier to discuss than formal mathematical problems. 'One can talk about their structure, one can talk about their development, their relation to one another, and to the original problem'.[15] Using Logo many children enjoy discussing mathematical concepts, and through articulating thoughts and sharing ideas much of the most important learning takes place.

Powerful implementations of Logo at the time of writing (1983) are not widely available on popular microcomputers in Britain, and are only available to all children in a small number of American schools. Floor-turtles are rarer still. It is a feature of the pace of change that by the time this book is published the picture may be very different: fuller Logos and turtle-like devices (such as the 'BBC Buggy') may be commonplace. Even fairly limited versions of turtle-drawing offer a number of advantages to the young learner: they can still provide a 'microworld' within which to explore concepts of space, angle, number, pattern and variables, and can offer a focus for collaborative discovery. However, only the more powerful versions offer the independently moveable 'sprites' which allow children both to create their own video games and to explore major physical concepts in a 'frictionless' world (an exploration which would be quite impossible without a computer, and very difficult without a language such as Logo).

In view of the tendency for many popular articles to make exaggerated claims, however, it may be worth adding that Logo cannot perform educational miracles. In MIT's Brookline Project (1979), despite a regular four hours per week in using Logo, two of the sixteen 12-year-olds involved did not learn to program, and some of the others developed only limited competence.[16] In another study, undertaken at Syracuse University, New York State, with children from 9 years old, some children seemed to gain little from the experience, finding the activity too demanding. The younger children found it very difficult to build up procedures. Researchers concluded that the child's developmental level was a major factor and that the level of thinking required tended to be roughly that which one might expect of 11-year-olds.[17] A floor-turtle with a pictorial 'button-box' instead of an alphanumeric keyboard has been used with children between the ages of 3 and 5 years old in studies by Perlman[18] and Gregg.[19] These studies have shown that although such children may easily play with the turtle, they cannot build up procedures, which is the key to its usefulness as a thinking-tool. Helen Finlayson at the University of Edinburgh has commented that the level of thinking required (and the usefulness of a familiarity with left and right) suggests that this system is probably more suitable for children from about the age of seven.[20]

Despite the advantages of Logo the strengths of turtle drawing for young children can sometimes become frustrations for an older child. Mark, a 12-year-old in an English middle school, observed that 'it's not all that interesting because all you're doing is drawing shapes and learning how to program a thing to draw shapes'. Although it is true that most children have access only to weak imitations of the purely graphical aspects of Logo, there is certainly a problem here. Once a child with even a fuller version of Logo becomes familiar with procedures and graphics it can be difficult for a child to discover some of the more sophisticated possibilities of the language. Very few children with access to suitable versions of Logo learn to manipulate text at all, for which indeed, there is little working space in memory in most current versions (although the memory limitations may have been solved almost as soon as these pages are printed). These difficulties may simply mean that children may need support from people with more experience of the language or of mathematical concepts – an older child or an adult. This doesn't mean that the adults have to provide the children with Logo exercises to do: Logo is a highly stimulating environment for children and adults to learn together. In a powerful version of the language there is a great deal to challenge even university students, and it would be a pity if the identification of Logo with children were to lead adults to forget that they are learners too.

Many of the widespread imitations of Logo could be described as special-purpose tools rather than general-purpose programming languages. The blurring of the distinction raises the issue of when a programming language is *not* a programming language, and when the user is programming the computer as opposed to using a program (however open-ended). Where high-level tools allow users to create their own programs they are referred to as authoring languages. PILOT, for instance, is an authoring language used to create instructional programs. Where the user is prompted to provide data (as in the business software called THE LAST ONE, and my own ADVENTURER) the tool is probably more accurately described as an authoring *system*. Such authoring languages and systems are a compromise between the versatility of a general-purpose programming language and the ease of use of a special-purpose program offering a menu of options.

Jim Levin has argued that the spread of such tools, acting as 'construction kits for programs' calls into question the value of learning general-purpose programming languages. Certainly where time is critical and the structure is at least adequate for one's purposes authoring systems may be convenient tools, but by their very nature they narrow one's range of options, lessen one's freedom in design, and, as someone else's framework, reflect someone else's priorities. Only if you write a program rather than simply use an authoring system are you able to explore alternative methods of solving a problem. 'Educational' authoring systems, for instance, frequently either tend to encourage or *will only allow* the creation of instructional sequences in a multiple-choice format. So, whilst it is surely desirable for children and adults to use high-level tools when they suit their purposes, if we discourage the learning of general-purpose programming languages on the grounds that such tools will meet all our needs, we will be responsible for creating the technocratic elite which will turn the rest of us into consumers.

We need to provide children with the opportunities to learn to use the computer as a tool for their own purposes – to release their inventive potential. Programming languages, authoring systems and other content-free tools can provide microworlds which children can control and explore, and their adventure of discovery is ultimately of far greater importance than whether or not they become proficient programmers. Whether they will enjoy such opportunities in a supportive environment depends entirely on the trust and vision of their parents and teachers.

6

Tomorrow and Tomorrow
and Tomorrow

Just as all education springs from some image of the future, all
education produces some image of the future.
Alvin Toffler[1]

Schools will not last for much longer unless they become far more
responsive to change and more open to radical restructuring. In an
era of rapid technological and social change we all need to have a
strong consciousness of the future. If parents and teachers are to
help children to cope with the world as they find it we must
ourselves adopt provisional images of the near-future. Three of
many strands which may provoke thought are concerned with the
future of printed books, the humanizing of computers and the
eventual disappearance of schools.

The future of the frozen word

Some of the functions of words on paper as a source of reference
are rapidly being fulfilled more efficiently by electronic media.
Systems which make it possible to display and retrieve information
on modified televisions (referred to as 'videotex') are clearly
capable of providing a more flexible medium for certain kinds of
public information which need to be constantly updated: news,
weather, sports results, travel information, food prices,
entertainment guides, and so on. In addition, as access to the
technology for the electronic storage of major encyclopaedias
becomes more publicly available, it is likely that 'tapping it out' will
replace 'looking it up' in a far wider range of routine reference
searches in which the need is for fast and specific information.

Where the need is to study such information the 'frames' could also be printed out as pages to be perused at leisure.

The technical fact that electronic media can perform (sometimes even better) some of the functions of books and newspapers does not mean that the latter will wither away. Television has not replaced newspapers, and there seems little point in transferring conventional fiction to electronic media. People will always need a medium which 'had the same words on it that it had when they read it the first time', as Asimov puts it in his story of a world without books.[2] Without such permanent records, we might find ourselves victims of the Orwellian vision of a Ministry of Truth, in which history is constantly being rewritten, and inconvenient facts disposed of in the 'memory hole'.

This should not blind us to the new possibilities which electronic media open up for us. In books, information is frozen in a particular arrangement, which is only partially counteracted by the rare aid of a good index. In an electronic medium such pathways through the content are necessarily far more important, offering the reader a greater sense of involvement in the process of use. At present, the potential of the medium in this respect has hardly been recognized, but current developments begin to show some of the ways in which the traditional relationship of reader to text may be shifted.

Two such developments are the 'Dynabook' and 'interactive fiction'. The concept of the Dynabook owes its origin to one of the most imaginative innovators in the field of computing, Alan Kay, currently director of research for Atari. It refers to a prototype personal computer, ultimately to be the size of a pocket notebook, which allows users to store, retrieve and manipulate the content of its vast store of words, pictures and animations using a powerful language called Smalltalk. Experimental Dynabooks allow users not only to find material by using existing concept indexes, but also to add their own cross-references and comments, to highlight words and to add subtitles. Browsing is made easier through a system of 'windows' which make it possible to compare one item with another. Such dynamic encyclopaedias led Dr Chris Evans to write that 'the world is about to move on from the era where knowledge comes locked up in devices known as books . . . In the era it is about to enter, the books will come down from their shelves, unlock and release their contents, and cajole, even beseech, their owners to make use of them.'[3]

'Interactive fiction' is an application of similar principles to fictional narrative.The current implementations of the concept on microcomputers give only a flavour of the idea. Some interactive stories, for instance, allow the reader to determine events by making decisions at key points: she would be 'branching' through a 'tree' of pre-prepared episodes. Elementary examples of such stories simply allow the reader to choose one of a series of numbered actions which would lead to unforeseen consequences: such structures have already been achieved in books with numbered paragraphs.[4] More sophisticated versions on microcomputers allow her to contribute comments to the dialogue which may or may not affect the development of the story. The adventure fantasy series known as the ZORK TRILOGY, which allows the reader to participate in the plot, sold about 100,000 copies in the US in 1982. Also developed in the US, Andee Rubin's program STORYMAKER (Bolt Beranek and Newman, 1982) shows another direction for development: users are able to add their own episodes to such a branching story, which may not seem particularly creative from the perspective of mature writers, but which is a liberating concept for young readers.

Electronic text, whether informational or fictional, is likely to be enriched by the increasing availability of 'interactive videodiscs'. Such discs, currently used in some commercial television replay systems, when linked with microcomputers, have already made it possible for a computer-based simulation of the Tacoma Bridge disaster to draw on film footage and audio commentary. Professor Wallace Feurzeig (co-developer with Papert of Logo) has described the way in which videodiscs could be used to transform readers of a story into actors in a drama, with, for instance, full visuals of a drive through the streets of San Francisco following one's decisions as to which way to turn.[5] In the long term the advent of powerful speech input facilities on microcomputers may lead to this particular application eschewing text altogether in order to heighten its attraction for the home entertainment market. Such a system, however, is more likely to be a challenge to the passivity of television than to printed fiction, which will remain a far more personal reading medium in view of its portability and cost.

Thus it would seem probable that whilst the book will not be replaced by electronic substitutes, the range of relationships between text and reader is likely to be extended by the new media. Words on paper will have become as representative of the full power and range of the use of words as still photographs are of the complete scope and potency of visual images.

The humanizing of computers

We already have computers which can produce speech, can recognize spoken words, and can be programmed to participate in simple dialogues. All these features will eventually come to be incorporated in personal computers. Given our tendency to attribute human characteristics to inanimate objects, it may be all too easy to treat the computers of the near future not only as conscious beings but as 'friends'.[6] Technologists and toy-makers will increasingly appeal to our tendency to humanize the computer by 'softening' the hardware as well as the software. Such developments could have considerable implications for the young learner.

Young children readily ascribe feelings and motives to inanimate objects. Piaget demonstrated that up to around 6 years of age children can consider anything to be conscious, and even moral: 'naughty' rugs, for example, can trip them up. Later, the criterion of movement becomes more significant; later still allowances are made for objects moved by people. Eventually, from around the age of 12 the child usually comes to regard only humans, animals and plants as being 'alive', although degrees of 'animism' survive into adult life.

Animism towards computers is reinforced by some kinds of software for children: for instance when reference is made to the computer as 'I', and where the names of the users are employed. Some teachers contribute to this by encouraging children to add faces and limbs to the monitor or to a floor-turtle. A 5-year-old girl, tired of losing in a tic-tac-toe (noughts and crosses) game, eventually asked 'How old is that computer?'. Dr Mary Humphrey reports that 'Some older children are also hesitant to play games against the computer 'because it might cheat' (Richard, 11) or 'it already knows the answers' (Andrea, 11). Such comments suggest that children see computers as 'knowing'.[7] Using present-day technology children can soon grow out of viewing the computer as a conscious being. A 9-year-old might easily think that 'The computer works like a person', but it is possible for an eleven-year-old to realize that 'A computer can't react like a human brain, with emotions.'[8] Older students are more conscious of the dangers: Paul (15) observed that 'I don't think computers should be used for correcting creative work . . . A computer . . . does not know the person who is doing the work.'

However, children would be only too happy to have the computer as a 'friend'. Even at 10, Jeff commented that he would like to 'have it talk with me and solve personal problems', and Satomi, at 11, said only a little more coolly, 'I would like to talk with it and discuss my problems so the computer can give its opinion'.[9]

As computer technology develops, and the capability for emulating human characteristics becomes more widely incorporated, there may be more cause for concern in the 'relationship' of children to their personal computers. The phenomenon of people getting 'hooked on' computers from their early teens is now well-known. These computaholics – often known as 'hackers' – may come to associate with computers more than with other people. As this phenomenon becomes more widespread amongst children it may be as well for us to bear in mind an observation by John Holt: 'There's a difference between a machine which increases our power in the real world and one which becomes a substitute world'.[10] Neil Frude paints an astonishing picture of the ways in which the personal computer could develop:

> It would perhaps be programmed to use the human contact as model and thus come to share the same figures of speech, phrasing and slang as its owner. It could also be made to enquire about the meaning of words which it did not understand and could incorporate these into its own vocabulary . . . It would be programmed to exhibit a gentle probing curiosity and would be able to build up a picture of the user's interests, opinions, preferences and past history . . . The rather shy and hesitant machine who [sic] entered the user's home for the first time might a few days later be chatting away with apparent ease and unconcern. . .[11]

This is a perfectly feasible scenario within the lifetimes of our children, and we should not avoid thinking about it precisely because of its disturbing implications. Seymour Papert, speaking in London recently, warned that 'the dependence of children on their parents and their siblings is probably integral to their emotional and social development. Fooling about with that link is, I think, very, very dangerous . . . I think we could easily turn up a generation of psychotic children . . .'.[12]

When will schools disappear?

Some commentators have speculated that the spread of more powerful computers could lead to the disappearance of schools. Such observers fall into two camps: the 'instructors' and the deschoolers.

The 'instructors' believe that education is essentially training. They argue that computers are more efficient than teachers in providing 'individualized' instruction. Therefore these educators dream of a future in which computers provide instruction in every child's home. The British inventor Sir Clive Sinclair has declared that 'the day will dawn when computers will teach better than human beings, because they can be so patient and so individually attuned. It [sic] will replace not only the Encyclopaedia Brittanica but the school.'[13]

For some parents who have been conditioned to regard education as 'taking the medicine because it's for your own good', computer-based instruction may well seem to be an attractive way of sugaring the pill. For those who own a home computer, there are countless computer programs dealing with 'basic skills' which offer the 'motivating' advantages of sound and graphics, as well as the instant 'feedback' which such activities seldom receive in school. When parents who are dissatisfied with the 'progress' their children are making in schools also find themselves with more time on their hands because of enforced leisure, it is possible that some may want to opt out of sending their children to school in favour of home-based computer instruction. It is also possible that it may prove to be politically expedient to make it easier for at least a percentage of the time a child normally spends in school to be spent in this way.

Speaking at a recent conference on alternative education in Britain Ronald Meighan, a sociologist at Birmingham University's Faculty of Education, foresaw a move towards what he called 'flexi-schooling'. This might involve 'contracts between parents and school based on 100 per cent, 75 per cent, 50 per cent, 25 per cent or almost nil time in school according to home circumstances at a particular time'. Already Lewknor primary school in Oxfordshire encourages parents to take their children home for an afternoon's project work each week. Ronald Meighan saw the new technology as being a major factor in bringing about such a change. 'In quite a short period of time, five or ten years perhaps, the majority of homes are likely to be equipped as sophisticated information retrieval centres, whilst schools, starved of the necessary funds, will do no more than replace old text books.'[14]

Some deschoolers see the computer as a potential agent of change on quite different grounds from those of parents and educators emphasizing its 'instructional' advantages. The emphasis is on providing children with opportunities to learn rather than making formal teaching easier to accept. Seymour Papert sees the computer as a powerful tool which can be used to help children to become more independent learners:

> The model of successful learning is the way a child learns to talk, a process that takes place without deliberate and organized teaching . . . I see the classroom as an artificial and inefficient learning environment that society has been forced to invent because its informal environments fail in certain essential learning domains, such as writing or grammar or school math. I believe that the computer presence will enable us to so modify the learning environment outside the classroom that much if not all the knowledge schools presently try to teach with so much pain and expense and such limited success will be learned, as the child learns to talk, painlessly, successfully, and without organized instruction. This obviously implies that schools as we know them today will have no place in the future.[15]

It is perhaps worth pausing briefly to consider the usual response to such declarations. By the time children are mid-way through secondary schooling even they are liable to respond by asking 'What about socialization?' This has actually happened to me many times during discussions at a 'progressive' secondary school. Papert's own response is worth hearing. He writes: 'Nothing enrages me more than when people criticise my criticism of school by telling me that schools are not just places to learn maths and spelling, they are places where children learn a vaguely defined thing called socialization. I know. I think schools generally do an effective and terribly damaging job of teaching children to be infantile, dependent, intellectually dishonest, passive and disrespectful to their own developmental capacities.'[16] Nevertheless, as one primary school teacher commented, socialization 'does not simply mean conforming to the wishes of adults – it does to some extent imply social interaction, especially with peers'.[17] The quality of interaction between children in classrooms – and consequently in school playgrounds – may not always be ideal, but (as Isaac Asimov highlights in his story 'The Fun They Had') a vision of isolated children plugged into home terminals and starved of a variety of opportunities to learn and play with other children is a real cause for concern.

I pursued the issue with primary-school children of 11 and 12 at Bradwell Village County Combined School in Milton Keynes. Here is an extract from the discussion:

MARK[12] Children who learned at home would have to have someone with them to get them to ask the computer what sort of questions . . .

ASTRID[12] If they had this vast database that the computer knew absolutely everything, then the ones that stayed at home would sort of learn more much quicker. And then they'd, sort of, mature much quicker because then they'd get more responsible and then they'd know more. So the children at school who'd been given a couple of maths cards to do they would be miles behind the ones on the computer . . .

EMMA[11] There's one more thing that you won't learn in school: when you're learning at home you'll learn about independence – you'll learn to cope on your own.

MARK And when you get outside into the big world then there'll be a lot of people around you and you'll wish you had your little computer with you – you'd need it.

EMMA Independent doesn't mean on your own all the time. Independent means you can cope on your own but you like to be with other people as well.

One may only hope that these children's championship of autonomous learning will survive their secondary schooling. At least their discussion shows the value of this kind of interaction for learning.

The most famous advocate of the deinstitutionalization of education is Ivan Illich, whose book *Deschooling Society* was published in 1971. Papert wrote in 1979 that he sympathized with Illich's perspective but expressed his own view that 'his proposals are totally utopian without a look at education through the prism of computer culture'.[18]

Ivan Illich had already argued in 1973 (before the appearance of microcomputers) that technology was being used 'mainly to increase the power and decrease the number of funnels through which the bureaucrats of education, politics and information channel their quick-frozen TV dinners. But the same technology could be used to make peer-matching, meeting and printing as available as the private conversation over the telephone is now.'[19] Peer-matching refers to a communications network which would make it easy for people to advertise offers and requests to share in particular learning activities. Certainly regional computer networks could make such matching easier. As Anthony Adams and Esmor Jones comment, 'the implications of this for the organisation of a society in which knowledge is a commodity to be shared with others rather than transmitted through a downward hierarchy is a thought-provoking one which could have economic as well as intellectual possibilities'.[20]

Technology may make such developments administratively feasible but the change required to make them happen is of an ideological and political nature rather than a technological one. Structural changes are necessary if alternatives to institutional education are to be more than simply minority options. With the prospect of schools losing their monopoly the large corporations are already moving into education. They have set up their own 'education services' and are producing heavily subsidized 'learning packages' more lavish than any that the impoverished schools can produce for themselves. In Britain, the oil company BP has just produced a seductive computer-based simulation package dealing with oil spillage from a tanker, and called, aptly enough, SLICK (reducing the politics of technology to a game in which the options are simply how best to cope with environmental consequences). And it was the UK Education Programmes Department of the computer firm IBM which recently published a poster entitled 'Will your children's children go to school?'. As Illich comments, 'proponents of recorded, filmed, and computerised instruction used to court the schoolmen as business prospects; now they are itching to do the job on their own'.[21] The wholesale deinstitutionalization of education in a society in which the power-structure and attitudes to education remain much as they are today invites the danger of substituting one disempowering curriculum for another, with even less checks on inequity.

The liberatory use of computers, as with any technology, can be frustrated by the existing limitations of the technology, a failure to perceive potential applications or a social pattern which tends to lead it to be used in support of the status quo. In the past, the technological barrier was the most significant. Illich and Papert have shown that it cannot be blamed solely on a failure of the imagination. It is possible that the computer itself could have a role in our resolution of the only remaining problem.

Presently, the dominant pattern of educational provision in western society involves an imposed system maintaining an uneasy balance between parents, their offspring, 'professionals', a central bureaucracy and the industrial complex. But the threat to the existing pattern of work posed partly by the limits to our current exploitation of resources, and partly by telecommunications and computers at least points to the need to develop more localized alternatives, with conditions negotiated by all the people involved for their own benefit and that of the whole local community. In such circumstances meaningful occupation, child-care and play could once more be integrated. If we remain alive to the issues, the computer – until now largely hijacked by institutional education as an 'educational' technology in the narrowest sense – could find a convivial role as a major means of supporting a society in which learning was not regarded as something separable from living.

7

A Tool for Change?

The reasonable man adapts himself to the world; the unreasonable man persists in trying to adapt the world to himself. Therefore all progress depends on the unreasonable man.

George Bernard Shaw[1]

We have explored some alternatives to the hospital model of education represented by the use of computers as mechanical instructors. These have included some kinds of games and simulations, content-free tools for the child as writer or researcher (such as word-processors and information-handling systems) and programming languages such as Logo which can release the potential of children as inventors. It has been suggested that all these examples illustrate possibilities which may extend the capabilities of young learners. If this is so, why is it that in most British and American schools computers are far more likely to be found used as electronic blackboards, page-turners, workbooks or testing devices, which restrict the potential both of children and computers? When teachers who have computers at home are asked what they use their own computers for they tend to list word-processing, information-handling and programming among their major uses. They seem to have little difficulty in finding software and programming languages to meet their own needs. But it is widely suggested that there is a shortage of suitable software for children. For some this may simply mean that the range of software for programmed instruction is not as comprehensive as they might like. Many justly argue that to use the computer as a tool requires children to have far more access to computers than is currently the case in schools. But it may also mean that children are not considered capable of handling the general-purpose tools which adults currently use. Such tools may indeed be badly-designed for easy use, but do children require different kinds of word-processors, information-handling systems and programming languages, or are we simply awaiting tools which are good enough for users of any age? The cost of computers will continue to fall, and the problem of access will soon not be the major barrier to children's use of computers as tools (although children will probably continue to have greater access to microcomputers outside rather than inside schools). Also, a wider range of imaginative people are likely to become involved in software design. But these two factors alone will not necessarily lead to any change of direction: they could lead simply to more and more attractively presented instructional programs. I suggest that the critical change required is one which need not await such developments: a revolution in attitudes – attitudes to computers, children and learning.

Attitudes to computers

Until parents, teachers and children become more conscious of what computers can and cannot do, commercial interests will persuade children to see them as video-games machines and parents to accept them as prescriptions, whilst institutional pressures may force teachers to use them as child-processors.

Surveys in recent years have shown that the vast majority of people would in fact agree that the computer is a tool (see Table 1). But in general most people would seem to think that it is best suited for doing repetitive tasks. This tends to imply that they see the computer as being a special-purpose tool with limited applications – 'just like a hammer' – rather than a general-purpose tool which can be made to behave in any way we can define. The more recent figures suggest that people have begun to question that the use of computers need necessarily be confined to repetitive tasks. This may suggest that over the last few years our greater exposure to computers in a variety of applications in daily life has had a significant effect on our attitudes to what computers can do.

One of the most difficult concepts to grasp is that computers need not be 'computers'. One example of this which is particularly relevant to young learners is the use of the computer as if it were a special-purpose laboratory instrument. One can now obtain appropriate interfaces and software to allow microcomputers to be used as simple but serious laboratory instruments. Fast and attractive visual feedback makes them suitable for children as well as adults to record, analyse and display 'real-time' data from many kinds of sensors. Young investigators can use such devices to perform experiments in science and engineering, on topics such as

Young Learners and the Microcomputer

Survey of Attitudes Towards Computers

	(1) US/Gy Adult 1975 N=300 Y% N%	(2) USA Teach 1976 N=162 Y% N%	(3) USA CStud 1982? N=38 Y% N%	(4) UK GPubl 1983 N=138 Y% N%	(5) UK Teach 1983 N=37 Y% N%
Computers are a tool, just like a hammer or lathe	73 15	77 8	95 3	59 32	81 16
Computers are best suited for doing repetitive, monotonous tasks	80 10	54 17	47 32	51 41	24 59
Computers are beyond the understanding of the typical person	25 62	30 47	21 58	41 49	14 81
Computers make mistakes at least 10% of the time	10 77	30 38	0 84	14 62	11 57
Programmers and operators make mistakes, but computers are, for the most part, error free	67 19	55 25	82 11	78 9	89 5
Computers isolate people by preventing normal social interactions among users	19 62	30 33	13 61	36 41	38 43
Computers will improve education	87 6	64 9	74 3	77 12	65 5

Notes

1 From David Ahl: 'Survey of public attitudes toward computers in society' in *The Best of 'Creative Computing'* (Creative Computing Press, 1976), pp.77-9. This group consisted of people of over 20 years of age in both the US and Germany (data collected in 1975).

2 From Dr David Lichtman: 'Survey of educators' attitudes toward computers', in *Creative Computing*, January 1979, pp.48-50. This group consisted of teachers and student teachers (data collected in 1976).

3 From Randy Ellsworth and Barbara Bowman: 'A 'Beliefs about Computers' Scale Based on Ahl's Questionnaire Items', in *The Computing Teacher*, December 1982, pp.32-4. This group consisted of undergraduate students majoring in Computer Science and taking an advanced programming course. 29 were males and 9 were females. The date of the survey is not given.

4 A survey made in Central Milton Keynes in November 1983 by students at Stantonbury Campus. 35% of the sample had no experience of using computers.

5 A small survey of primary and secondary level teachers in two schools using computers in Milton Keynes.

light level, humidity, air-flow, water-flow, velocity and acceleration. Microcomputer-based instrumentation (MBI) can provide them with much more detailed and sophisticated experiences of observing natural phenomena than has previously been possible. Children with a personal computer and the appropriate peripherals can have a mini-laboratory at home or in the smallest village school. Data and phenomena can be made easier to understand because of the variety of visual presentations that are possible on a microcomputer. Such instrumentation also offers a far less distracting laboratory environment.

But perhaps more significantly, the advantages of this kind of imstrumentation make it far easier for children to direct their own investigations. The psychologist Jean Piaget declared: 'I'm convinced that one could develop a marvellous method of participatory education by giving the child the apparatus to do experiments and thus discover a lot of things by himself'.² The feedback which microcomputer-based instrumentation can supply (allowing a user, for instance, to read the acceleration as she pulls an object along) means that experiments may be shorter and simpler than so much 'discovery learning' in science. Such an approach therefore becomes feasible even within institutional education. One sixth-grade student in the US using microcomputer-based instrumentation to make graphs of acceleration discovered a personal version of Newton's Second Law of Motion which was stated as 'to get acceleration, you have to keep pulling'. Using such equipment, preliminary findings suggest that children *ask more questions*.³

Such a use of computers also makes an intuitive approach much more productive. It may offer a chance for those who tend to feel more comfortable with 'bottom-up' strategies to explore 'subjects' in which the encouragement of structural and analytical approaches has led many to believe that 'science doesn't suit them'.

Computers and learning

A broader understanding of the capabilities of computers may help us to re-assess their potential for extending children's strengths as thinkers. When people become more aware that computers need not be inflexible machines, perhaps it will be easier for us to talk of 'computer-extended thinking' instead of 'computer-assisted instruction'. Using a computer offers a rare opportunity for a child to gain an immediate enjoyment from the exercise of her intellect. To the observer this may at times seem a 'passive' activity when a child spends hours at a time apparently doing little more than tapping at a keyboard, scribbling a few notes or staring into space, with 'nothing to show for it' until weeks later. When she finally erupts into ecstasy over a pattern on the screen we may find it difficult to resist thinking that she could have created something like that in minutes with a Spirograph. But the invisible thinking in which such children engage may be exploiting capabilities for which the computer has become a catalyst – capabilities which have previously been unknown or ignored. And who really believes that we are already providing children with adequate opportunities to release their full potential as thinkers? I have already referred, in Chapter 5, to Margaret Donaldson's point that to be a successful learner one needs to be sufficiently self-aware to control one's thinking. Piaget, in *The Grasp of Consciousness*, argued that awareness tends to develop when something causes us to stop and consider the possibilities before acting. Computers can provide a supportive environment for considering possibilities. As was suggested in Chapter 3, drafting our ideas with a word-processor may actually encourage us to explore alternatives. And experimental simulations (discussed in Chapter 2) may allow us to see what might happen to a particular model of a process if we do this or that. And when children can build their own models, however limited, they can enjoy the God-like experience of exploring alternative worlds. This is not to deny the importance of pure fantasy for children. One of the benefits of computers, quite different from the free play of fantasy, may be in helping children to learn how to slow down their thinking – to reflect on what they really mean.

'Computer-extended thinking' implies for me the use of computers to help us to explore things in ways which would otherwise be difficult if not impossible. For teachers to approach the computer by trying to think about how they can do more 'efficiently' what they do already is hardly the most fruitful avenue of exploration: we discovered in Chapter 1 where that can lead. Comparative studies of conventional educational practice versus the use of computers are misleading because they invariably ignore the new capabilities that computers provide. As Jacquetta Megarry writes, 'If the computer's role is artificially restricted to that of an electronic blackboard or super-calculator, the experiment will probably demonstrate that it has no more effect on the quality of learning as measured by pre- and post-tests than you would expect of a blackboard or calculator'.[4]

Microelectronic technology is obviously not a necessary aid for learning. 'Sometimes,' said 11-year-old Emma, 'I think a book's better.' But technology includes pens and books, and reading and writing have been described by Jack Goody as the 'technology of the intellect'. Without wishing to suggest that I am complacent about overdependence on technology, it may be worth reminding ourselves that to reject it entirely is to attempt to return to an oral culture. We live in a world in which microelectronic technology plays a major part: we cannot ignore it, and to spurn its usefulness is to look at our hands and wish they were paws. What we can do is to assert our right to use it as and when we choose, and refuse to allow 'technological imperatives' to dictate what we must do with it. This will involve thinking about what kind of uses might suit us and our children best, and knowing enough to be critical of what powerful forces thrust upon us. The checklist for choosing software provided in Appendix 1 may form a practical starting-point for thinking about such issues, but the reader's own framework, evolving from the needs of individual children, will inevitably be of far more value. The questions we ask ourselves, like the ways in which we choose to use computers, will depend on our attitude to learning.

Attitudes to learning

If we expect learning to be imparted and to require a teacher, the phenomenon of a child using a computer for her own purposes will not seem like learning. The priorities for children to learn might be listed as follows:

> That there should be a supportive environment; That suitable tools (such as pens and books) should be available; That there should be access to competent practitioners of the craft that the children want to acquire (not necessarily adults); That there should be opportunities to learn together with others (not necessarily children).

For instance, in learning to program, assuming that the activity is accorded value by parents or teachers, the other priorities for children would be: having easy access to a computer, a suitable programming language and reference sources; being able to watch and consult someone who has some competence in programming; and having the chance to share their learning experiences with other people. Everett Reimer suggested that 'the best skill models are frequently those who have just learned a skill'.[5] Certainly a recent study by Karen Shiengold and others have shown that children learning programming are particularly likely to identify their peers as resources for help in the classroom.[6] Having a teacher as such is not essential, although I would emphasize that the *support* of sensitive and observant adults is vital as a first priority. As Dr Henry Olds and others put it, 'whilst the intellectual benefits of tools and tool-makers are potentially great, the intellectual demands for using them are also great'.[7] We need to be conscious of how a child is coping with a computer: the more open-ended the tool, the bigger the chance not only for her to extend her power as an inventive thinker, but also for her to drown with frustration.

Despite the 'revolution' in education which was supposed to have occurred in the late 1960s and early 1970s, the order of priority of the conditions for learning given above is quite unlike what one finds in all but a handful of British primary schools. Usually the highest priority is still accorded to *teaching*. However, the very existence of powerful learning tools *outside* schools will gradually help to undermine the identification of learning with formal instruction. It will be many years yet before learning becomes such an integral part of daily life that we will be able to dispense with schools. But in the meantime the role of teacher needs to shift from that of instructor to that of consultant, and parents need to become more involved in the role of partners in learning with their children (for which they require not only the time which increased leisure may bring them, but support from the existing educational establishment). As more children gain access to personal computers it will become patently absurd for parents and teachers to behave as if the process of education can be regarded as separable from learning in the home and in the community at large. Teachers can't ignore the fact that 'the fastest growing segment of the educational software market is educational packages for the home – a segment that's increasing at the rate of 71 percent a year'.[8] They may be disturbed by the poor quality of much of this software, but that, at least, should be a spur for them to share with parents their experiences of using computers with children.

The computer challenges our expectations about children's capabilities and challenges our attitudes to our own. As we are repeatedly confronted with the fact that children can rapidly acquire considerable professional expertise with computers, many adults – especially some teachers – feel threatened. Some react by attempting to 'keep ahead' whilst others, fearing comparison, do not attempt to learn, and may even use the ploy of declaring how clever children are with such gadgets. Far rarer is the teacher or parent who, never regarding her role as that of a fount of knowledge, is accustomed to being a partner in discovery with younger learners. This is not to deny the value of her broader experience: indeed it is precisely this that may make her participation of particular value to children. For instance, the adult's use of talk in problem-solving may be a powerful model for the younger child. For the locus of control to remain close to the child, it is this kind of relationship between adults and children which is required when using computers: a relationship in which the concept of 'authority' is irrelevant. The very meaning of 'adult' and 'child' is questioned when both regard themselves as learners.

Those aware of Papert's emphasis on self-directed learning sometimes agonize about 'when to intervene' whilst children are using Logo. Surely the answer is for adults to behave as responsive individuals rather than as teachers. Just as any reasonable person would do her best to direct someone asking how to get to the railway station, so if a child wants to know how to do something, or looks lost, and an adult happens to know a way, it makes sense to offer it. But we may need to learn from Karen Sheingold's study of children's social behaviour when using computers: 'Many wanted to be able to ask more expert children for help when they needed it, but did not want to work with children who might dominate the interaction with the computer.'[9] An adult should be more capable of being sensitive to such needs.

Playful participation might involve 'brainstorming' together: producing ideas which nobody 'owns' in order to find solutions for problems somebody genuinely wants to solve. Both children and adults could gain from the joint design of programs which meet their needs. Children are unlikely to see any purpose in using computers unless they see that adults use them in similar ways, and no-one uses 'drill-and-practice' programs in the 'real world'.

Strategies for adaptive thinking

Writers such as Alvin Toffler have alerted us to the recency and acceleration of social and technological change, but we have hardly begun to examine its implications for young learners. Few, however, would disagree with the assertion that 'our schools face backwards towards a dying system, rather than forwards to the emerging new society. Their vast energies are applied to cranking out industrial men – people tooled for survival in a system that will be dead before they are.'[10]

In an era of such rapid change, there is a desperate need for all of us – not just children – to develop flexible strategies for learning. Children are particularly vulnerable to manipulation by increasingly powerful media. If they are to survive in the 'Information Society' which has been ushered in by the dramatic developments in microelectronics, they need to be able to rely on a range of methods of self-defence.

● As institutional bureacracies grow, everyone who is to remain free must have confidence in her own ability to solve problems, and should actively enjoy thinking and asking questions.

- In a constantly changing world, no-one should allow themselves to be fooled into believing that anyone is an expert. As Marshall McLuhan once said, 'An expert is a person who stays put'.
- Anyone who wishes to learn should be capable of exploring a range of thinking styles and should know how to make the most effective use of her own strengths.
- We need to realize that there is no 'best method' of tackling a problem and must be prepared to seek out alternative methods. If we are to continue learning we must accept that we could have produced other solutions, or could make existing ones more effective.
- In a global village in which we are increasingly dependent on each other we must value collaboration. In learning together the experience of every individual is worth sharing, and we need to be willing to offer help as well as to seek it.
- Learners cannot afford to be afraid of making mistakes. They need to feel free to change their minds. We must expect to have to 'debug' our thinking.
- A consciousness of relativity is a powerful ally against dogmatism. We need to be conscious of variable factors, to weigh one against another and to realize that 'it all depends . . .'
- We need to be conscious of the various media and of the ways in which they can affect what we do with them.
- We need experience in interpreting data, and must continually question the accuracy of sources of 'information'.
- We must not feel obliged to produce quick solutions, and should allow children the time they need to think things out for themselves.
- If our thinking is to remain imaginative we must keep alive the spirit of play. We need to be speculative: to ask ourselves, 'What might happen if . . .?'

As we have seen, an imaginative use of computers with young children could help us to create an environment in which such attitudes and strategies could flourish. But such a consequence is far from inevitable: without active discrimination against the processing of the child and in favour of computer-extended thinking it is highly unlikely.

Postscript

I began to write this postscript at a minute past eleven o'clock on the morning of Wednesday 30 November 1983. And as I wrote, I became acutely conscious of the way in which the printing and publishing of the book freezes my ideas in time. Thanks to its storage on disc, my personal version of the text has been able to change from day to day since I began to write it a few months ago. It has undergone many major transformations throughout the period I have been working on it: the very fact that I have been using a word-processor has encouraged me to keep changing the text to reflect my changes of mind. Suddenly, as I am faced with its publication in conventional form I must accept that I can no longer use the text you are reading to explore my own thinking: it is a map of the past. This is frustrating for the author, but it does at least offer the reader (whose role I may now share) a chance to explore the same territory in the full knowledge that her own exploration is inevitably better informed.

Appendix I

Choosing Software: a Checklist

'MULTIPLOY combines the excitement of an arcade game with the challange (sic) of learning and practicing (sic) arithmetic skills. The game was developed for children between the ages of 4 and 11, but adults like it too.' [Advertisement]

'I think the game Multiploy is not worth playing. The way its crudely put together makes it look like a crumby game (which it is). The couple of times you play it it seems fun(ish) but after that it gets uninteresting. The keyboard to screen response is really slow and the noises it makes are silly.' [Ben, aged 11]

[Quoted in *Chiltern Computing*, No. 11, October 1983, p. 3]

Other people's reviews and sample runs are useful, but of course there is no substitute for users trying out the software personally. It is not usually possible to obtain software on approval from the producers, but the rapid spread of local 'user-groups' offers an opportunity to see some of the more popular software. Remember that software which may not have been designed as 'educational' software may yet have educational potential, and that the label 'educational' is no guarantee that it is any better than a 'workbook'.

The checklist assumes that you have already ascertained that the program in question will in fact run on the computer you intend it for, and that you have any additional attachments that the program may need (e.g. an appropriate printer for a word-processor).

The following is a very general and personal checklist designed with both parents and teachers in mind. You will need to adapt and add questions yourself. Most of the questions are open-ended, so the list does not lend itself to evaluation by counting the number of times you answer 'Yes'. They are intended merely to focus attention on particular issues.

CONTENT

- What might a child learn from using the program? This may have nothing to do with any stated aim.
- Is it worth learning?
- Is this an effective way to learn it? Does this method justify the expense?
- How might it affect a child's attitude to learning?
- How might it affect a user's attitude towards computers?
- Would the child see a real purpose in the activity?
- Does it present the user with a challenge?
- Is the program likely to stimulate creativity?
- Is it likely to be fun to use?
- Would it appeal to both sexes?
- Is it likely to make users want to explore the matter further?
- Can it be used in a variety of ways?
- Would it be worth using many times?
- Is it suitable for use by more than one person at a time? If so, is it likely to encourage discussion and the sharing of ideas?

PRESENTATION

- Is there an interesting, attractive and appropriate use of colour, graphics and sound?
- Are the frames uncluttered and easy to read?
- Is the use of language appropriate for the intended users?
- Is the pattern of the program easy for a child to grasp?
- Is it clear to the user what she is expected to do at any point?
- Is it easy for the user to move around the program? (E.g. is there a 'menu-page' of options to which she can easily return?)
- Are there too many options?
- Is any 'page-turning' under the user's control?
- Is the program tolerant of accidental key-presses?
- Is it easy for the user to correct her typing errors?

NOTES

- Are there clear notes explaining the program?
- Is the intended purpose explained adequately?
- Is there a simple guide to loading and running the program?
- Is a typical 'run' of the program explained?
- Are there helpful ideas for use and further activities?
- Are you shown how to adapt the program?
- Is a telephone inquiry number given?

Appendix 2

Some Further Reading
Note This list consists of many of the recent books on computers and the young learner which are accessible to parents and teachers; a list of recommended reading would be much shorter.

Adams, Anthony, and Esmor Jones *Teaching Humanities in the Microelectronic Age* (Open University Press, Milton Keynes, 1983)

Chandler, Daniel *Micro-Primer Study Text* (Tecmedia, Loughborough, Leicestershire, 1982)

Chandler, Daniel (ed.) *Exploring English With Microcomputers* (Council for Educational Technology, London, 1983)

Coburn, Peter, Peter Kelman, Nancy Roberts, Thomas F. Snyder, Daniel H. Watt and Cheryl Weiner *Practical Guide to Computers in Education* (Addison-Wesley, Reading, Mass., 1982)

Daines, Derrick *Micro-Primer Reader* (Tecmedia, Loughborough, Leicestershire, 1982)

Doerr, Christine *Microcomputers and the 3 Rs* (Hayden, Rochelle Park, NJ, 1979)

Elder, Ron, and Russel Wills *Microcomputers in Primary Education* (Dundee College of Education, Dundee, 1982)

Ellingham, David *Primary Education and Computers – A First Handbook* (Castle House, Tunbridge Wells, Kent (in press))

Garland, Roy (ed.) *Microcomputers and Children in the Primary School* (Falmer Press, Lewes, Sussex, 1982)

Geoffrion, Leo D., and Olga P. Geoffrion *Computers and Reading Instruction* (Addison-Wesley, Reading, Mass., 1983)

Gill, Peter *Microcomputer-Assisted Learning in the Primary School* (Ward Lock Educational, London, 1983)

Hammond, Ray *Computers and Your Child: A Plain Language Guide for Parents* (Century, London, 1983)

Hawkins, Jan, Karen Sheingold, Maryl Gearhart and Chana Berger *Microcomputers in Schools – Impact on the Social Life of Elementary Classrooms* (mimeo, Bank Street College, New York, 1982)

Jones, Ron *Microcomputers – Their Uses in Primary Schools* (Council for Educational Technology, London, 1980)

Jones, Ron (ed.) *Five of the Best – Computer Programs in Primary Schools* (Council for Educational Technology, London, 1982)

Maddison, Alan *Microcomputers in the Primary School* (Hodder & Stoughton, Sevenoaks, Kent, 1983)

Maxwell, Beryl *Logo Report – A Term with a Floor-Turtle* (mimeo, Advisory Unit for Computer-Based Education, Hatfield, Herts., 1982?)

Meredith, Maurice, and Brenda Briggs *Bigtrak Plus* (Council for Educational Technology, London, 1982)

Moursund, David *Introduction to Computers in Education for Elementary and Middle School Teachers* (International Council for Computers in Education (ICCE), Eugene, Oregon, 1981)

Moursund, David *A Parent's Guide to Computers in Education* (International Council for Computers in Education (ICCE), Eugene, Oregon, 1983)

Noss, Richard *Starting Logo: Interim Report of the Chiltern Logo Project* MEP Chiltern Regional Centre, c/o Advisory Unit for Computer-Based Education, Hatfield, Herts., 1983)

Obrist, A.J. *The Microcomputer and the Primary School* (Hodder & Stoughton, Sevenoaks, 1983)

O'Shea, Tim and Self, John *Learning and Teaching with Computers – Artificial Intelligence in Education* (Harvester Press, Sussex, 1983)

Olds, Henry F., Judah L. Schwartz and Nancy A. Willie *People and Computers – Who Teaches Whom?* (Education Development Center Inc, Newton, Mass., 1980)

Papert, Seymour *Mindstorms – Children, Computers and Powerful Ideas* (Basic Books, New York, 1980; Harvester Press, Brighton, 1980)

Papert, Seymour, Daniel Watt, Andrea diSessa and Sylvia Weir *Final Report of the Brookline Logo Project, Part II and III, Logo Memos No.53/54, A I Memos No.545/546*, (Artificial Intelligence Laboratory, Massachusetts Institute of Technology, 1979)

Sheingold, Karen, Janet Kane, Mari Endreweit and Karen Billings *Study of Issues Related to Implementation of Computer Technology in Schools* (mimeo, Bank Street College, New York, 1981)

Taylor, Robert P. (ed.) *The Computer in the School: Tutor, Tool, Tutee* (Teachers College Press, Columbia University, New York, 1980)

Wayth, Peter A. *Using Microcomputers in the Primary School* (Gower, Aldershot, 1983)

Appendix 3

Classroom Computer News Intentional Educations Inc., 51 Spring Street, Watertown, MA 02172

Computers, Reading and the Language Arts (CRLA) Dr Gerald H. Bloch, Editor, PO Box 13039, Oakland, CA 94661

Computing Teacher 135 Education, University of Oregon, Eugene, OR 97403.

Creative Computing PO Box 789-M, Morristown, NJ 07960

Educational Computer Magazine PO Box 535, Cupertino, CA 95015

Educational Technology 140 Sylvan Avenue, Englewood Cliffs, NJ 07632

Electronic Education Electronic Communications Inc., Suite 220, 1311 Executive Center Drive, Tallahassee, FL 32301

Electronic Learning Scholastic Inc., 902 Sylvan Avenue, Box 2001, Englewood Cliffs, NJ 07632

Journal of Computer-Based Instruction ADCIS, Computer Center, Western Washington University, Bellingham, WA 98225

Journal of Educational Technology Systems Baywood Publishing Co. Inc., 120 Marine Street, Box D, Farmingdale, NY 11735

Microcomputers in Education Queue Inc., 5 Chapel Hill Drive, Fairfield, CT 06432

T H E *Journal* (Technological Horizons in Education), PO Box 992, ACTON, MA 01720

Turtle Talk Harvest Publishing, 118A Magazine Street, Cambridge, MA 02139

Appendix 4

Major Software Sources

Britain

ACORNSOFT 4a Market Hill, Cambridge CB2 3NJ (Atom, BBC, Electron)

APPLIED SYSTEMS KNOWLEDGE (ASK) London House, 68 Upper Richmond Road, London SW15 (BBC, Commodore VIC)

ADVISORY UNIT FOR COMPUTER-BASED EDUCATION (AUCBE) see 'Other Useful Addresses', Appendix 5 (BBC, RML)

CAMBRIDGE MICRO SOFTWARE Cambridge University Press, The Edinburgh Building, Shaftesbury Road, Cambridge CB2 2RU (BBC, RML, Sinclair Spectrum)

FORMAT EDUCATIONAL SOFTWARE Linden Lea, Rock Park, Barnstaple, Devon EX32 9AQ (BBC)

GINN & COMPANY LTD Prebendal House, Parson's Fee, Aylesbury, Bucks HP20 2QZ (Apple, BBC, Commodore PET)

ILEA COMPUTING CENTRE John Ruskin Street, London SE5 0PQ

ITMA COLLABORATION see 'Other Useful Addresses', Appendix 5 (Apple, BBC, RML)

LONGMAN PRIMARY MICRO SOFTWARE Longman Micro Software Unit, Longman House, Burnt Mill, Harlow, Essex CM20 2JE (BBC, RML)

MICROCOMPUTERS AND PRIMARY EDUCATION (MAPE) see 'Other Useful Addresses', Appendix 5 (Apple, BBC, Commodore PET, RML, Sinclair Spectrum)

MICROELECTRONICS EDUCATION PROGRAMME (MEP) see 'Other Useful Addresses', Appendix 5 (BBC, RML, Sinclair Spectrum)

MICROCOMPUTER USERS IN EDUCATION (MUSE) see 'Other Useful Addresses', Appendix 5 (Apple, BBC, Commodore PET, RML)

NEWMAN COLLEGE PRIMARY SOFTWARE c/o Roger Keeling, Newman College, Bartley Green, Birmingham B32 3NT (BBC, RML)

TECMEDIA LTD., 5 Granby Street, Loughborough, Leicestershire LE11 3DW. Publishes the MEP Micro-Primer in-service training package for primary schools (BBC, Spectrum, RML)

North America

BOLT BERANEK AND NEWMAN INC (BBN) see 'Other Useful Addresses', Appendix 5 (Apple)

BRODERBUND SOFTWARE 1938 Fourth Street, San Rafael, CA 94901 (Apple, Atari)

CREATIVE COMPUTING see 'Relevant Journals', Appendix 3 (Apple, Atari, TRS-80)

THE LEARNING COMPANY 4370 Alpine Road, Portola Valley, CA 94025 (Apple)

McGRAW-HILL BOOK COMPANY School Division, 1221 Avenue of the Americas, New York, NY 10020 (Apple, Commodore PET, TRS-80)

MINNESOTA EDUCATIONAL COMPUTING CONSORTIUM (MECC) see 'Other Useful Addresses', Appendix 4 (Apple, Atari)

QUEUE 5 Chapel Hill Drive, Fairfield, CT 06432 (Apple, Commodore PET, TRS-80)

SCHOLASTIC INC. 904 Sylvan Avenue, Englewood Cliffs, NJ 07632 (Apple, Atari, Commodore PET, TRS-80, Texas Instruments)

SOFTSWAP Anne Lathrop, San Mateo County Office of Education, 333 Main Street, Redwood City, CA 94063 (Apple, Atari, Compucolor, Commodore PET, TRS-80)

SPINNAKER SOFTWARE CORPORATION 215 First Street, Cambridge, MA 02142 (Apple, Atari, IBM, Commodore 64)

TEACHING TOOLS: MICROCOMPUTER SERVICES 3659 Ross Road, Palo Alto, CA 94303 (Apple, Atari)

TERRAPIN INC. 380 Green Street, Cambridge, MA 02139 (Logo for Apple, Commodore PET)

Appendix 5

Other Useful Addresses

Britain

Advisory Unit for Computer-Based Education (AUCBE), Endymion Road, Hatfield, Herts. AL10 8AU

Association for Computer-Assisted Learning (ACL), Institute for Educational Computing, St Martin's College, Lancaster

BBC Microcomputer System, c/o Vector Marketing, Dennington Estate, Wellingborough, Northampton NN8 2RL. Suppliers of the BBC Microcomputer system

British Logo User Group (BLUG), c/o Pam Valley, Shell Centre for Mathematics, School of Education, University of Nottingham, University Park, Nottingham NG7 2RD

Cambridge Language Arts Software Services (CLASS), c/o Esmor Jones, Director, 197 Henley Road, Caversham, Reading RG4 0LJ

Computer Education Group, North Staffordshire Polytechnic Computer Centre, Blackheath Lane, Stafford

Computers in Education as a Resource (CEDAR), Imperial College Computer Centre, Exhibition Road, London SW7 2BX. Central source of information on computers in education

Computers in Education Group, Department of Artificial Intelligence, University of Edinburgh, Scotland EH1 2QL

Computers in the Curriculum (CIC), Chelsea College, University of London, Hudson Building, 552 Kings Road, London SW10 0UA

Council for Educational Technology (CET), 3 Devonshire Street, London W1N 2BA. Publishes many useful booklets on computers in education

Economatics, 4 Orgreave Crescent, Dorehouse Industrial Estate,

Handsworth, Sheffield S13 9NQ. Suppliers of the 'BBC Buggy'
Guild Organization Ltd, OU Film Library Department, Guild
House, Peterborough, Cambridgeshire PE2 9PZ. Suppliers of a
videocassette version of 'Talking Turtle', a widely acclaimed
television programme in the BBC Horizon series, co-produced
by the Open University and the BBC
Informatics Education Unit, Department of Education, University
of Southampton, Southampton
Institute for Educational Technology, The Open University, Walton
Hall, Milton Keynes, Bucks MK7 6AA
Investigations in Teaching with Microcomputers as an Aid (The
ITMA Collaboration), College of St Mark and St John, Derriford
Road, Plymouth PL6 8BH and The Shell Centre, University of
Nottingham, University Park, Nottingham NG7 2RD. Producers
of an in-service training package, 'Micros in the Primary
Classroom' (published by Longmans)
Jessop Microelectronics Ltd, Unit 5, 7 Long Street, London E2
8HN. Suppliers of the Edinburgh University floor-turtle for
Apple, BBC, RML and Sinclair microcomputers (with OK Logo)
Loughborough Primary Micro Project, Department of Education,
University of Technology, Loughborough, Leicestershire.
Responsible for some excellent programs in the Ladybird-
Longman Micro Software series (available from Longmans)
Microcomputers and Primary Education (MAPE). Secretary: Mrs
G.E. Jones, 76 Sudbrooke Holme Drive, Sudbrooke, Lincoln
LN2 2SF
Microcomputer Users in Schools (MUSE). PO Box 43, Hull
Westhill College, Weoley Park Road, Selly Oak, Birmingham
B29 6LL
Microelectronics and Computers in Education (MACE). Ian Glen,
West Midlands Regional Centre, Four Dwellings School,
Dwellings Lane, Quinton, Birmingham B32 1RJ
Microelectronics Education Programme (MEP), Cheviot House,
Coach Lane Campus, Newcastle upon Tyne NE7 7XA
Microwriter Ltd, 31 Southampton Row, London WC1. Producers
of the Microwriter hand-held word-processor
Open University Micros in Schools Project, The Open University,
Walton Hall, Milton Keynes MK7 6AA. Publishes an in-service
training package for teachers
Scottish Microelectronics Development Programme (SMDP), 74
Victoria Crescent Road, Glasgow G12 9JN

North America
Acorn Computer, c/o Harvey Lawner, 12 Alfred Street, Woburn,
Massachusetts. Agent for the BBC Microcomputer system

Association for the Development of Computer-Based Instructional Systems (ADCIS). Dr Gordon Hayes, Executive Director, Miller Hall 409, Western Washington University, Bellingham, WA 98225

Bolt, Beranek and Newman Inc (BBN), 50 Moulton Street, Cambridge, MA 02238. Base for an imaginative software research and development project

Center for Children and Technology, Bank Street College of Education, 610 West 112th Street, New York, NY 10025. Has published a number of useful research reports

Computer Education Resource Coalition (CERC), Lesley College, 29 Everett Street, Cambridge MA 02238

Computers, Learners, Users, Educators Association (CLUES). Henry J. Petersen, Executive Director, 50 Nellis Drive, Wayne, NJ 07470

International Council for Computers in Education (ICCE), 135 Education, University of Oregon, Eugene OR 97403

Microcomputer Education Applications Network (MEAN), 256 North Washington Street, Falls Church, VA 22046

Minnesota Educational Computing Consortium (MECC), 2520 Broadway Drive, St Paul, MN 55113

National Institute for Microcomputer-Based Learning (NIMBL). Stanley Silverman, President, 348 Plymouth Avenue, Brightwaters, NY 11718

Northeast Regional Exchange (NEREX), 101 Mill Road, Chelmsford, MA 01824

Northwest Regional Educational Laboratory (NWREL), 500 Lindsay Building, 300 SW 6th Avenue, Portland, OR 97204

Technical Education Research Center (TERC), Computer Resource Center, 8 Eliot Street, Cambridge, MA 02138

Young People's Logo Association (YPLA). James H. Muller, 1208 Hillsdale Drive, Richardson, TX 75081

Appendix 6

Schooling Systems in the Britain and the US

AGE	BRITISH PRIMARY		US ELEMENTARY	GRADE	AGE
12	Middle	[Secondary]	[Middle]	6	12
11		Junior	Intermediate	5	11
10				4	10
9				3	9
8	First		Primary	2	8
7		Infant		1	7
6				K	6
5		Pre-school	Pre-school		5
4					4
3					3

Note The age boundaries in both systems are subject to local variations.

Notes to the Text

Preface
1 Alan Ellis, *The Use and Misuse of Computers in Education* (McGraw-Hill, 1974), p.42.
2 George Orwell, *Nineteen Eighty-Four*, (Penguin, 1954), Appendix ('The Principles of Newspeak').
3 Marshall McLuhan and Quentin Fiore, *War and Peace in the Global Village*, (Bantam, 1968), p.18.

Chapter I A Mechanical Instructor?
1 Lewis Carroll, *Alice in Wonderland* (Macmillan 1865), Chapter IX.
2 In *Micro-Primer Case Studies* (audio cassettes) produced by Julian Coleman (Tecmedia, 1982).
3 Peter Wayth, *Using Microcomputers in the Primary School* (Gower, 1983), p.58.
4 In *Micro-Primer Case Studies*.
5 Peter Wayth, *Using Microcomputers*, p.16.
6 Mary Humphrey, ' All the scientists in the world smushed into one : What kids think of computers' in *Creative Computing*, April 1982, p.98.
7 Peter Gill, *Microcomputer-Assisted Learning in the Primary School* (Ward Lock Educational, 1983), p.21.
8 Frank Smith, 'Demonstrations, engagememt and sensitivity: The choice between people and programs' in *Language Arts*, 28, No.6, September 1981, p.638.
9 Patrick Suppes, 'The uses of computers in education' in *Scientific American*, September 1966, p.207.
10 Christine Doerr, *Microcomputers and the 3 Rs* (Hayden, 1979), p.121.

11 J.A.M.Howe and B. du Boulay, 'Microprocessor-assisted learning: Turning the clock back?' in N.Rushby, *Selected Readings in Computer-Based Learning* (Kogan Page, 1981), p.121.

12 The bar-chart of 'Types of Program' was derived from one presented by David Zacchei at a conference of the North-East Regional Exchange (NEREX), held in Albany, New York State in May 1983.

13 (UK) *National TRS-80 Users Group Newsletter*, 2, No.11, May 1981, p.20.

14 Virginia Makins, 'Getting brains buzzing', in the *Times Educational Supplement*, 24 April 1981.

15 *Atari Guide to Computers in Education* (1982), p.11.

16 Arthur C. Clarke, *Profiles of the Future* (Pan, 1973), p.216.

17 From a chart presented by David Zacchei at the NEREX conference mentioned in note 12. See also Andee Rubin, 'The computer confronts language arts: Cans and shoulds for education' (mimeo, Bolt Beranek and Newman Inc., Cambridge, Mass., 1982), p.6-7 to be published in *Classroom Computers and Cognitive Science*, ed. Alex C. Wilkinson (Academic Press, 1983).

18 Jonathan Swift, *Gulliver's Travels* (1726), (Collins, 1953), Part 3, Chapter 5, p.204-5.

Chapter 2 The Learning Game

1 Lewis Carroll, *Alice in Wonderland*, (Macmillan, 1865), Chapter X.

2 See Ronald King, *All Things Bright and Beautiful? A Sociological Study of Infants' Classrooms* (John Wiley, 1978), Chapter 2.

3 Catherine Garvey, *Play*, (Open Book, 1977), p.10.

4 Iona and Peter Opie, *Children's Games in Street and Playground*, (Clarendon Press, 1969).

5 Ibid.

6 Aldous Huxley, *Brave New World*, (Chatto and Windus, 1932), Chapter 3.

7 See Ron Jones, *Microcomputers: Their Uses In Primary Schools*, (CET, 1980), p.86.

8 Quoted in Sara Kiesler, Lee Sproull and Jacquelynne S.Eccles, 'Second Class Citizens' in *Psychology Today*, March 1983, p.43.

9 Edna Mitchell, Chair of the Education Department at Mills College in California, speaking at a conference on 'Video games and human development' held at Harvard in 1983.

10 Gregory Yob, in *The Best of 'Creative Computing'*, Volume 1, p.267.

11 A simple version of the game ANIMAL can be found in David Ahl's BASIC *Computer Games*, (Creative Computing, 1979).

12 Recorded at Bradwell Village County Combined School, November 1983.

13 Seymour Papert, 'Computers and Learning' in Dertouzos and

Moses (eds.), *The Computer Age: A Twenty-Year View*, (MIT Press, 1980), p.76.

14 *Mary Rose: Teacher's Notes*, (Ginn, 1982), p.3.

15 Douglas Barnes, James Britton and Harold Rosen, *Language, The Learner and the School*, (Penguin, 1971), p.132.

16 Research being conducted (1983/4) by Mallory Heatley at Bradwell Village Combined School in Milton Keynes

17 Karen Sheingold, Janet Kane, Mari Endreweit and Karen Billings, *Study of Issues Related to Implementation of Computer Technology in Schools*, (mimeo, Bank Street College, New York, 1981); Jan Hawkins, Karen Sheingold, Maryl Gearhart and Chana Berger, Microcomputers in Schools: Impact on the Social Life of Elementary Classrooms (mimeo, Bank Street College, New York, 1982).

Chapter 3 Words which Dance in Light

1 John Holt, *Freedom and Beyond* Penguin (1972), Chapter 11, and *How Children Learn* Revised edition, Dell (1983); Herbert Kohl, *Reading, How to* Penguin (1974); Frank Smith, *Writing and the Writer* Heinemann (1982).

2 Connie and Harold Rosen, *The Language of Primary School Children* Penguin (1973), p.85.

3 Bob Lawler, quoted in *Growing Without Schooling*, 31 (1983), p. 14 from an article in *The Boston Review*, June 1982.

4 Frank Smith, *Writing and the Writer*, p.94.

5 Seymour Papert, 'Society will balk, but the future may demand a computer for each child' in *Electronic Education*, 1982.

6 Seymour Papert, *Mindstorms: Children, Computers and Powerful Ideas*, Harvester Press (1980), p.30.

7 Bernard Banet, 'Computers and early learning' in *Creative Computing*, September/October 1978, p.92.

8 Illustration from *Byte*, April 1982, p.34.

9 Monty Python, *Matching Tie and Handkerchief* (audio record) (Charisma, 1973).

10 Stephen Marcus of the University of California at Santa Barbara in a lecture at the Spring convention of the National Council for the Teaching of English, Seattle, April 1983.

11 Colette Daiute, 'Writing, creativity and change', in *Childhood Education*, March/April 1983, p.227.

12 Ibid., p.230.

13 Ibid., p.227.

14 Stephen Butler in a letter to the author, November 1983.

15 Mike Sharples in a personal communication with the author, November 1983.

16 Alvin Toffler, quoted in G.Courter, 'Word machines for word

people' in *Publisher's Weekly*, February 13th 1981.

17 Frank Smith in conversation with the author at the University of Victoria, British Columbia, on 27 April 1983.

18 Virginia N.Bradley, 'Improving students' writing with microcomputers' in *Language Arts*, 59, No.7, October 1982, pp.736-7.

19 Mike Sharples, personal communication (see note 15).

20 See Mike Sharples, 'A construction kit for language' in Daniel Chandler (ed), *Exploring English with Microcomputers*, (Council for Educational Technology, 1983), pp.51-8.

21 Judy Wedman, 'Software: What's in it for Reading?' in *Journal of Reading*, April 1983, p.642.

22 Frank Smith in a lecture on 'Learning to read like a writer' at the International Reading Association convention, Anaheim, California, May 1983.

Chapter 4 Getting Wise to 'Information'

1 Quoted in Birkenhead's *Life of F.E.Smith*, Chapter 9.

2 Daniel Chandler, 'An Antidote to Infomania' in *Infostorms*, ed. Ann Irving (Council for Educational Technology, 1984).

3 Joel Moses, 'The computer in the home' in Moses and Dertouzos (eds.), *The Computer Age: A Twenty-Year View* (MIT Press, 1980), p.13.

4 Isaac Asimov, *A Choice of Catastrophes*, (Arrow, 1981), p.332.

5 'The Bryanston Seminar' was sponsored by Bryanston Audiovision and held at the University of Cambridge from 23-25 October 1981. FACTFILE was one of many ideas put forward by a group of primary school teachers and teachers of the humanities in secondary schools and the University's Department of Education. The seminar did in fact turn out to be a turning-point in the evolution of attitudes to computers and the humanities in Britain. A report can be found in a book by the two lecturers whose inspiration the seminar was: Anthony Adams and Esmor Jones, *Teaching Humanities in the Microelectronic Age*, (Open University Press, 1983).

6 Alistair Ross, 'Data-processing in primary science using micro-LEEP' in *Computers in Primary Schools Newsletter*, no. 1, p.9. See also Alistair Ross, 'Conkers and Statistics in the Classroom' in *Acorn User*, December 1983, pp.99-105.

Chapter 5 Learning to Control the Computer

1 Lewis Carroll, *Alice Through the Looking-Glass*, (Macmillan, 1871), Chapter VI.

2 For a study of the device demonstrating its ineffectiveness in 'teaching' spelling see C.D.Terrell and O.Linyard, 'Evaluation of electronic learning aids: Texas Instruments' SPEAK AND SPELL'

in *International Journal of Man-Machine Studies* (1982), 17, pp.59-67.
3 *Bigtrak* is manufactured by Milton Bradley.
4 Maurice Meredith and Brenda Briggs, *Bigtrak Plus*, (Council for Educational Technology, 1982).
5 Seymour Papert, *Mindstorms: Children, Computers and Powerful Ideas* (Harvester Press, 1980), p.viii.
6 Dr Carl Smith, 'Trends and attitudes in instructional materials' in *Education Monographs*, Indiana University, June 1983. Results from a more recent survey appeared in the December 1983 edition of *Educational Technology*. All US school districts were contacted between July and September. 68 per cent of all public schools had computers (325,000 computers), and 62 per cent of elementary schools had them (110,000 computers). Elementary schools using microcomputers had tripled to 31,991 in the preceding 12 months (so the average elementary school had 3.5 computers).
7 By November 1983 the Department of Industry had received applications for computers from 16702 primary schools under the 'Micros in Primary Schools' scheme. There are 22,523 primary schools in England and Wales, attended by 4,087,471 children. Excluding the lunch-break, the average length of a primary school day is around 5 hours.
8 Heather Govier, 'Programming – how to face this difficult issue' in *Acorn User*, April 1983, p.46.
9 Peter Davies, 'The primary curriculum/micro interface: implications for in-service education and resource provision' in *Microcomputers and Children in the Primary School*, ed. Roy Garland, (Falmer Press, 1982), p.96.
10 Margaret Donaldson, *Children's Minds*, (Fontana, 1978), pp.88-9.
11 W.Feurzeig, P.Horowitz and R.S.Nickerson, *Microcomputers in Education*, Report No. 4798 (Bolt Beranek and Newman, Cambridge, Massachusetts, 1981), p.11.
12 Derek Bunyard, Letter to the Editor, in *Chiltern Computing Primary Newsletter*, No. 2, January 1983, p.2.
13 Richard Noss, 'Logo' in *Chiltern Computing Primary Newsletter*, No. 2, p.3.
14 T.J.Fletcher, 'Microcomputers and mathematics in schools: a discussion paper', Her Majesty's Inspectorate, Department of Education and Science (1983), p.10.
15 W.Feurzeig, P.Horowitz and R.S.Nickerson, *Microcomputers in Education*, p.41.
16 Seymour Papert, Daniel Watt, Andrea diSessa and Sylvia Weir, *Final Report of the Brookline Logo Project*, AI Memo Nos. 545/6; Logo Memo Nos. 53/4 (MIT, September 1979).
17 J.Statz *et al.*, *Logo Progress Reports* nos. 1, 2 and 3, Syracuse University, New York State (1972); and Folk, PhD Thesis,

Syracuse University (1972).
18 R.Perlman, 'Using computer technology to provide a creative learning environment for pre-school children', Logo Memo No. 24, (MIT, 1976).
19 L.W.Gregg, 'Spatial concepts, spatial names, and the development of exocentric representations', Technical Report, Carnegie-Mellon University (1978).
20 Helen Finlayson, 'Developmental levels in mathematical thinking', DAI Working Paper No. 132, Department of Artificial Intelligence, University of Edinburgh, February 1983.

Chapter 6 Tomorrow and Tomorrow and Tomorrow
1 Alvin Toffler, quoted in Benjamin D. Singer, 'The Future-Focussed Role-Image' in *Learning for Tomorrow: The Role of the Future in Education*, ed. Alvin Toffler (Vintage Books, 1974), p.19.
2 Isaac Asimov, 'The fun they had' (1954) in *The Best of Isaac Asimov* (Sphere, 1973).
3 Christopher Evans, *The Micro Millenium* (Viking Press, 1980).
4 See, for example, Cambridge University Press's *Storytrails* series.
5 Wallace Feurzeig in conversation with the author, Cambridge, Mass., 18 May 1983.
6 See Neil Frude, *The Intimate Machine*, (Century, 1983).
7 Mary M Humphrey, "All the scientists in the world smushed into one': What kids think about computers' in *Creative Computing*, April 1982, p.98.
8 Ibid.
9 Mary Humphrey, 'All the scientists', p.97.
10 John Holt in conversation with the author in Boston, Mass., May 1983.
11 Neil Frude, *The Intimate Machine*, p.138-9.
12 Seymour Papert, in a lecture in London on 4 September 1983, reported by Ray Hammond in 'God of Word Worlds' in the *Times Educational Supplement*, 16 September 1983.
13 Clive Sinclair, quoted in *Computing Today*, January 1983, p.29.
14 Ronald Meighan, quoted in the *Times Educational Supplement*, 29 April 1983.
15 Seymour Papert, *Mindstorms: Children, Computers and Powerful Ideas*, (Harvester Press, 1980), p.8-9.
16 Seymour Papert in the *Times Educational Supplement*, 5 March 1982.
17 Mallory Heatley in a letter to the author, November 1983.
18 Seymour Papert, 'Computers and learning' in Dertouzos and Moses (eds.), *The Computer Age: A Twenty-Year View*, (MIT Press, 1980), p.85.
19 Ivan Illich, *After Deschooling, What?*, (Writers and Readers

Publishing Cooperative, 1976), p.54. See also: Illich, *Deschooling Society*, (Penguin, 1973), p.89-98; Everett Reimer, *School is Dead*, (Penguin, 1971), p. 121; John Holt, *Instead of Education*, (Penguin, 1976), Chapters 4-5.

[20] Anthony Adams and Esmor Jones, *Teaching Humanities in the Microelectronic Age*, (Open University Press, 1983), p.119.

[21] Ivan Illich, *After Deschooling, What?*, *p.41*.

Chapter 7 A Tool for Change?

[1] George Bernard Shaw, *Man and Superman*, 'Maxims for Revolutionists'.

[2] Jean Piaget, quoted in Jean-Claude Bringuier, *Conversations with Jean Piaget* (University of Chicago Press, 1980).

[3] Robert Tinker, 'Can instrumentation improve teaching?' in *Hands-on*, Technical Education Research Centers, Cambridge, Mass., Fall 1981.

[4] Jacquetta Megarry, 'Thinking, learning and educating: the role of the computer' in *World Yearbook of Education 1982/3: Computers and Education*, ed. Jacquetta Megarry, David Walker, Stanley Nisbet and Eric Hoyle, (Kogan Page, 1983), p.24.

[5] Everett Reimer, *School is Dead*, (Penguin, 1971), p.118.

[6] Jan Hawkins, Karen Sheingold, Maryl Gearhart and Chana Berger, *Microcomputers in Schools: Impact on the Social Life of Elementary Classrooms* (mimeo, Bank Street College, New York, 1982).

[7] Henry F.Olds, Judah L.Schwartz and Nancy A.Willie, *People and Computers: Who Teaches Whom?* Education Development Center Inc., Newton, Mass., 1980), p.41.

[8] Trudy Bell, 'Computer literacy: the fourth R' in *Personal Computing*, May 1983, p.63.

[9] Hawkins, Sheingold, Gearhart and Berger, *Microcomputers in Schools*, p.16.

[10] Alvin Toffler, *Future Shock* (Pan, 1971), pp.360-1. See also Toffler's *The Third Wave*, (Pan, 1981).

Glossary of Terms Used in Educational Computing

Adventure game: a type of game originally developed on mainframe computers but now available as home entertainment software for most microcomputers. The players find themselves in environments which they 'explore' by typing in simple sentences.

AI: see artificial intelligence.

alphanumeric: characters which can be either letters or numbers.

animation: the process and effect of moving graphics.

applications: the problems to which computing techniques are applied.

artificial intelligence (AI): quasi-intelligent behaviour exhibited by computers or robots. The term is used to describe systems which can emulate quite closely human thinking processes such as reasoning, learning and self-correction. Also used to refer to the field of research concerned with developing and studying such systems.

assembly language: a low-level programming language which is close to the computer's machine-code and is consequently faster (useful, for animated graphics) and more space-saving than a high-level language such as BASIC. It is also far more difficult for the lay-user to understand. It uses mnemonics rather than recognizable words.

audio cassette: a standard cassette-tape which can be used for storing programs and data.

authoring language: a high-level programming language which enables those unskilled in writing programs in conventional programming languages (such as BASIC) to write a special-purpose program (for example, for computer-assisted instruction).

authoring system: software which prompts the user to provide data and then creates a special-purpose tool which will function as a program. Examples include the business system called THE LAST ONE and my own ADVENTURER (developed at Chelsea College with Jan Bright).

backing store: an external memory-store of larger capacity than the computer's built-in memory: for example, audio cassettes or floppy disks. For the long-term storage of programs or data.

back-up copy: a reserve copy of a program or datafile kept in case of loss or damage to the original.

BASIC: a simple high-level programming language using recognizable English words. Most microcomputers have BASIC built in. Different dialects are used for different types of computer, but programs written in a fairly standard subset of BASIC are not difficult to convert for a particular type of computer.

behaviourism: a psychological theory (associated particularly with B.F.Skinner) involving the analysis of observable behaviour and resulting in a theory of learning based on stimulus and response (conditioning).

bit: a binary digit (0 or 1). The smallest unit of computer storage.

bottom-up approach: a problem-solving strategy in which one begins by tackling small sections of the problem without first devising a clear overall plan. In programming this might involve building a program up from modules. See also top-down approach.

branch: part of a computer program or information-retrieval system where a choice is made between alternative routes through the sequence of frames or events.

BREAK: a key on computer keyboards which enables the user to stop the running of the program. Pressing this key in an unprofessionally written program might cause the program to crash.

bug: a flaw in a program resulting mainly from mistyping, inadequate thinking through of the logic of the program or misunderstanding of some aspect of the programming language being used. See also debugging.

byte: a group of bits (usually 8) used to represent one character of text. See also K.

CAD: see computer-aided design.

CAI: see computer-assisted instruction.

CAL: see computer-assisted learning.

CAL *package* (UK): a multi-media collection of learning materials on a specific topic, including one or more computer programs.

CAT: computer-assisted teaching – a synonym for computer-assisted instruction.

CBE, CBL: computer-based education/learning – a synonym for

computer-assisted instruction.

Central processing unit (CPU): the control centre of a computer, including the microprocessor, the arithmetic unit and the main memory. It is usually inside the keyboard unit in a microcomputer.

character: a symbol – for example, a letter, a number or a punctuation mark. Note: Spaces between words also count as characters.

chip: a common term for the tiny square wafer of silicon containing a single integrated circuit equivalent to thousands of transistors. It looks like a centipede when 'packaged'.

CMI, CML: see computer-managed learning.

cognitive psychology: a modern school of psychology which maintains that the mind does not merely react to stimuli but actively transforms the data it receives. Human learning and problem-solvingare referred to as 'information-processing'.

command: a direct instruction to the computer (typed by the user) which it carries out immediately (for example, RUN).

compatibility: software compatability: this term is used to refer to whether or not programs can be transferred and run from one computer to another; hardware compatability: refers to whether or not one piece of computer equipment will function in association with another.

computer: a fast, general-purpose electronic device for storing and manipulating symbols.

computer-aided design (CAD): the use of computers as tools to assist designers, draughtsmen and engineers in the design process.

computer-assisted instruction, computer-aided instruction (CAI): the use of computers to provide instruction or drill-and-practice. Widely used in the US to include what in the UK is referred to as CAL.

computer-assisted learning, computer-aided learning (CAL): the use of the computer to provide learning opportunities.

computer awareness: a term frequently used to describe an awareness of the uses and implications of the use of computers in general (not specifically in education).

computer education: the study of computers as opposed to educational computing.

computer-extended thinking: term used by this author to refer to the use of computers to help us to think about things in ways which would otherwise be difficult or impossible.

computer literacy: a term often used loosely to refer to an ability to operate computers (sometimes also including programming and/or computer awareness). Perhaps more logically used to refer to new dimensions of traditional literacy required by the computer medium, such as in screen-reading, writing with a word-processor and information retrieval.

computer-managed learning, CML, (UK) *and computer-managed instruction*, CMI, (US): the use of computers for monitoring, analysing and reporting on users' progress in individualized instruction.

computer system: a complete computer, including the CPU (often built into the keyboard), a VDU and backing store, as well as any other linked peripherals such as a printer.

conditional statement: a statement in a program telling the computer to do something only under certain conditions. For example, IF X = 2 THEN STOP.

content-free software: software in which the subject-matter is chosen by users, who must enter the relevant data themselves.

content game: an educational game in which the main intention is for users to learn about the subject-matter dealt with. See also process game.

control technology: directly controlling the operation of external devices or processes through the use of computers.

convivial: a term used by some writers to describe socially responsible technologies (derived from the writings of Ivan Illich).

corrupted: a term used to describe the state of a program or datafile on audio cassette or floppy disk, the contents of which have been damaged (often by magnetic fields) so that the program or data is unusable.

courseware: in the UK this term is commonly used to mean educational materials associated with the computer software (often print materials). In the US the term more commonly refers to the educational software itself.

cpl: characters per line.

cps: characters per second.

CPU: see central processing unit.

crash: a term used to refer to the condition when a program which is running comes to a premature halt, offering the user no obvious way of making it resume functioning.

crashproofing: a programmer's attempt to build safeguards into a program to ensure that users will not unwittingly crash it.

CRT: cathode ray tube (as in a television or monitor). In the US, used to mean VDU.

cursor: a symbol (sometimes flashing) shown on the screen to indicate where the next typed character will appear. It can often be moved around the screen by means of up, down, left and right arrows.

daisy-wheel printer: a computer printer which produces a variety of good-quality type because the plastic typeface 'wheels' are interchangeable. It is therefore widely used for commercial word-processing.

data: in computing, numbers, words or facts in a form suitable for storage in a computer.

DATA: a statement in a program identifying a line of data to be read by the computer and used in the program. Usually at the end of a program.

databank: a term sometimes used to refer to a database to which many people have access through terminals in different locations.

database: an organized collection of computerized data which can be searched for specific information.

datafile: recorded data organized in a consistent format (for example, name, address, telephone number) for use by a program.

data-processing: sorting or reformulating quantities of data in some way, usually with computer-based systems.

debugging: removing flaws from a program.

dedicated: an adjective used to describe a piece of hardware designed for a specific application. For example, a dedicated word-processor is one which is built as a word-processor rather than a computer which can also run word-processing software.

DELETE: a named key on many micros which, when pressed, deletes on the VDU the previous character typed on the keyboard.

descriptor: in an information retrieval system (especially bibliographic systems) the key concepts associated with individual records in a file, allowing the user to retrieve a file without knowing its contents (for example, an article on peace education might have the descriptor 'peace' even though the title did not include the word).

developmental level: refers to a stage in a child's development characterized by different patterns of behaviour and reasoning (from the theories of the psychologist Jean Piaget).

dialect: a version of a particular programming language with some unique variations.

discovery method (also *inquiry method* or *heuristic method*) : an approach to education in which the intention is for learners to play an active part in discovering something for themselves rather than passively accepting someone else's account of it.

disk (also *disc* or *diskette*) : see floppy disk.

disk drive unit: a device which reads from floppy disks into a computer. The disk revolves at high speed, and data is transmitted to and from it through read/write heads.

documentation: the print materials associated with a computer system or a computer program.

Documentation includes: the user manual for a particular computer (including technical information); program notes, listings, flow-charts and sample output (sometimes in UK misleadingly used to include associated learning materials).

dot matrix printer: a computer printer which forms characters from tiny dots made by needles hitting a ribbon.

drill-and-practice: a sequence of exercises intended to 'reinforce' learning.

Dynabook: 'a personal dynamic medium the size of a notebook . . . which could be owned by everyone and could have the power to handle virtually all of its owner's information-related needs' (Alan Kay and Adele Goldberg, 'Personal dynamic media' in *Computer*, 10, pp.31-41 (1977)).

editing facilities: computer functions which enable the user to make changes to text on the screen. The DELETE key is a simple editing facility.

educational computing: the use of computers for educational purposes as opposed to the study of computers.

electronic blackboard: a term used to refer to a type of program used by a teacher to provide a visual display for large group presentation.

electronic mail: the transmission of messages between computerized equipment, usually via the telephone line.

encoding: writing a computer program in the precise code of a programming language.

ENTER: a key on some computer keyboards performing the same function as RETURN.

error-trapping: including in a program ways of ensuring that unanticipated input does not cause the program to crash.

ESCAPE: a key on the keyboard of some computers allowing the user to stop a program running.

expert system: a program which uses the expert knowledge with which it has been provided to process solutions to formally-structured problems. For instance, an expert system might have been provided with specialist data and rules for answering questions on a topic such as plant identification.

field: in information retrieval, a defined part of a record in a datafile (for example, that which is set aside for a telephone number).

field length: in information retrieval, the possible number of characters in a field.

field name: in information retrieval, the heading used for a particular field (for example, NAME).

file: see datafile.

file name: a set of characters (with no spaces) used to identify a datafile. The file name may need to be used when it is loaded or saved.

firmware: a program resident in ROM.

floppy disk (also referred to as a *diskette*): a lightweight medium for the rapid storage and retrieval of programs and data. Rather like a small flimsy audio record. Coated with a magnetic material and enclosed in a square envelope within which it can revolve.

flow chart: a diagram representing the sequence of steps in a program or a problem.

frame: the contents of the visual display screen at any one time.

games paddle: see paddle.

graphics: pictures and diagrams created on a computer (as opposed to text). See also high-resolution and low-resolution graphics.

graphics tablet: a flat device which can be connected to a computer enabling the user to draw on it with a special pen and to see the result on the VDU screen.

hands-on: direct use of the computer keyboard.

hard-copy: printed computer output forming a durable record.

hardware: the physical units which constitute a computer system.

Hawthorne effect: usually refers to a tendency for the behaviour of the subjects of an experiment to be affected by the presence of observers. Sometimes used to mean simply a tendency for a technique (such as using computers) to work because of the novelty factor.

heuristic method: see discovery method.

hex (hexadecimal): a method of counting in base 16 used in assembly language programming. One byte can be represented by two hexadecimal symbols (for example, 45 (decimal) = 2D (hex)).

hierarchical database: a database based on a tree structure (q.v.) (see also database, relational database).

high-level language: a programming language closer to natural vocabulary than machine code.

high-resolution graphics: graphics capable of displaying fine lines.

holistic approach: sometimes used to refer to the importance of learning being seen in the context of experiences which cannot usefully be divided into 'skills'. Also used to refer to a top-down strategy (q.v.) and contrasted with a serialist approach (q.v.).

home computer: see personal computer.

IC: see integrated circuit.

implementation: the setting up of a program on a particular computer.

informatics: a term sometimes used to refer to the study of the way we manipulate information, and its social implications.

information: sometimes distinguished from data (which may not provide information) as data organised in some way which makes it meaningful.

information literacy: competence to cope with the efficient retrieval of data – particularly using computerized databases.

information processing: see data-processing and cognitive psychology.

information retrieval: searching large quantities of data for that which meets specified criteria.

information technology (IT): the technology associated with the communication, storage and retrieval of data.

input: the data or program fed into a computer.

input device: any peripheral used to feed data or programs into a computer. The most common manual input device is the keyboard. Alternative input devices commonly used by very young children include simplified keyboards, joystick controls and light-pens.

inquiry method: see discovery method.

instrumental understanding: a term derived from R R Skemp. Knowledge involving the memorisation of rules for particular kinds of processes without knowing why they work. This is the kind of knowledge which underlies 'skills'. See also relational understanding.

integrated circuit: a miniature electronic circuit made from a single piece of material. Often synonymous with chip.

interactive: in computing, usually used to refer to some kind of dialogue between computer and user. Misleading when applied to programs in which the user is simply prompted to answer 'yes' or 'no'.

interactive fiction: narratives displayed on the video screen of a computer, which allow the reader to intervene, either by choosing particular paths through a branching plot, or by entering dialogue or narrative of her own which may or may not cause such branching.

interface: the connection between two peripherals or computer systems.

IP: information provider. The name given to organizations paying for display space on British Telecom's Prestel viewdata system.

IT: see information technology.

joystick: a control device which can be connected to most microcomputers to allow the user to provide input without using the keyboard. Similar to the controls on table-tennis video game machines.

K: abbreviation for kilobyte, the unit in which memory size is measured (1024, or 2^{10}, bytes).

keyboard: a set of keys forming part of a computer system similar to those of a typewriter. The user's main means of communicating with the computer.

keypad: a set of calculator-like keys provided for convenience on one side of some computer keyboards (also called a numeric keypad); a hand-held remote-control device looking rather like a calculator but used in association with viewdata or teletext systems.

keyword matching: the identification of key words corresponding to a checklist stored in the computer program. A phrase common in

AI and information retrieval.

language: see programming language.

LCD *display*: a type of display based on liquid crystal diode technology. Widely used on pocket calculators and digital watches, with dark characters on a light background.

learning styles: a person's habitual approach to learning, thinking or problem-solving, such as serialist (q.v.), holistic (q.v.), impulsive or reflective. See also strategies.

line: one of the instructions or sequences of instructions to the computer in a program (numbered in BASIC).

line number: refers to the number of a line in a program. This is the number shown at the left of each line in a BASIC listing. It is conventional to number lines in tens – 10, 20, 30 etc.

LIST: a command which can be typed by the user to show a listing of the program on the VDU screen and sometimes also via a printer.

listing: a printed list of program instructions, usually produced by the computer printer.

LOAD, *loading*: a command used to transfer the contents of a program from an audio cassette or floppy disk into internal memory (RAM).

locking-up: a condition whereby the computer ceases to respond to any input for no apparent reason.

locus of control: used by this author to refer to where on an imaginary spectrum the control of an activity resides – close to the user or close to the computer program. Derived from Dr Jim Levin.

Logo: a high-level programming language designed for children by Wallace Feurzeig and Seymour Papert. Most well-known for its suitability for geometrical drawing, but with considerable potential for exploring concepts in physics as well as mathematics. The name itself was coined by Wallace Feurzeig.

loop: a function in a program allowing something to be done several times.

low-level language: a programming language close to that used internally by the computer itself, such as assembly language.

low-resolution graphics: primitive graphics where the image displayed is made up of square blocks rather than fine dots.

machine: what computer people call the computer.

machine code, machine language: the language that the computer can act on directly – a series of Os and 1s. Other programming languages have to be translated by the computer into machine code before they can be used.

machine independent: used to describe a program which will run on several types of computers.

mainframe computer: a very large (traditional) computer installation which can have numerous terminals connected to it.

MBI: see microcomputer-based instrumentation.

memory: a computer's store for data and programs. Usually used to refer to internal (immediate) memory – particularly RAM (but sometimes also ROM). Occasionally used to include external backing store memory, for example, audio cassettes or floppy disks.

memory size: the size of available RAM (immediate memory) on a particular computer. Only programs of this size or smaller can run on the computer.

menu: a part of a program shown on a VDU as a list of choices of action for the user. Each choice leads down a different branch of the program.

menu-driven program: a program in which the user can easily return to the menu (q.v.) to select an option.

microchip: see chip.

microcomputer (sometimes simply 'micro' in the UK): a small computer with a microprocessor (CPU) mounted on a board. Usually used to mean also the VDU and the backing store, although this might be more usefully described as a microcomputer system.

microcomputer-based instrumentation (MBI): the use of the computer as a laboratory instrument for recording, analyzing and displaying real-time data.

microprocessor: sometimes also used to mean microcomputer, but strictly, a CPU on a chip which can interpret and execute instructions in a small computer.

microworlds: a term used by advocates of the Logo programming language to mean a computer-based system for exploratory learning within a specified 'environment' such as 'turtle graphics'.

Microwriter: a British hand-held (battery-operated) word-processor with only six keys and a narrow LCD display. It can be plugged into a conventional monitor when a larger display is required and uses non-volatile memory.

mini-computer: a medium-size computer which is usually part of a larger system. Widely used in business applications.

modelling: testing hypotheses by building formal (mathematically-based) models of possible situations.

monitor: a television-like video display for computer output. Also a computing term referring to a technical means of monitoring the computer's internal operation.

multiple-choice question: a question followed by a series of alternative answers, only one of which is regarded as being valid.

natural language: ordinary conversational language. In computing, a field in artificial intelligence research in which programs are developed to allow users to communicate with the computer (usually via the keyboard) in everyday language.

network: any system consisting of a series of connected points. In computing, usually a system in which several computers are linked to each other or in which a number of terminals are connected to a computer.

neutrality of technology: the idea that we can separate tools from the interests which bring them into being and the use to which they are put.

non-volatile memory: see volatile.

OCR: optical character recognition. The direct reading of printed (and sometimes handwritten) text by a computer.

operating system: firmware which manages all the operations of the computer and its peripherals, interprets input and reports errors to the user.

operational understanding: being able to understand a concept and to apply it in a different context.

output: the data which a computer sends out for the user, usually via a VDU, a printer or a backing store.

paddle: see joystick.

PASCAL: a structured high-level programming language.

PC: see personal computer.

PCB: printed circuit board. The plastic board to which the electronic components of a circuit are attached, and linked by thin wires 'printed' on its surface.

peripherals: the input and output devices attached to the computer – for example, a VDU, an audio cassette-recorder and a printer.

personal computer (PC): a microcomputer system designed for, or widely used in, a domestic setting.

PILOT: a simple high-level programming language sometimes used for CAI. It is designed to allow teachers to write their own programs. It is particularly valued for the ease with which it can match a response with a series of alternatives provided by the program author.

pixel: the basic element used to create a video-display – a tiny dot of light.

playing turtle: in the context of using Logo, this phrase refers to the user pretending to be a floor-based turtle (q.v.), trying to walk through the exact movements which such a robot would need to perform to create a pattern which the user wants.

port: the place for the electrical connection of peripherals to a microcomputer.

portability: programs are portable if they can be implemented on several computer systems. This does not necessarily mean that the audio cassette or floppy disk will run on another computer, but that the program should run on other computers after being typed in from the listing.

power-up: switching on the various components of a computer system. There is sometimes a preferred order in which to switch on the equipment listed. This would be indicated in the manual for a particular computer.

printer: a device which can be connected to a computer to produce printed output.

print-out: see hard-copy.

problem-solving: thinking directed towards finding solutions to formal problems, as in mathematics and programming. G.Polya in *How to Solve It* (Doubleday, 1957) listed four stages: understanding the problem; devising a plan for its solution; executing the plan; reviewing the solution.

process games: educational games in which the main intention is for learners to acquire or extend particular learning strategies rather than their knowledge of the content.

processor: see microprocessor.

program: a complete sequence of precise coded instructions for the computer to make it perform a particular task. The original is typed into a computer, although subsequent copies may be loaded from audio cassette or floppy disk. In British usage, not to be confused with programme (as in 'a television programme' or 'a programme of activities').

program design: the process of deciding what a program is intended to do and what the user should see and do at each stage.

program development: the process of designing, programming, debugging and validating a program.

programmed instruction: a teaching method for individual instruction in which a precisely-defined sequence of steps must be followed.

programmer: anyone who encodes computer programs.

programming language: a set of coded instructions, together with the necessary syntax, allowing the user to control the computer. A variety of languages exist (such as BASIC and PASCAL), some of which were designed for specific purposes (LISP, for instance, was designed for artificial intelligence research).

program name: the name which may need to be used with some computer systems in order to save or load a program.

program specification: the detailed list of requirements given to a programmer so that he or she knows exactly what the program must do.

prompt: a character (often a question mark or a 'greater than' sign (()) displayed on the VDU screen indicating that the computer is waiting for the user to enter some data. Sometimes used to include a brief text prompting the user.

RAM: random access memory. Part of a computer's built-in memory store which temporarily stores programs and data. Usefully thought of as the computer's immediate memory. The contents are erased when the power supply is switched off.

READY: a word sometimes shown on the screen indicating that a computer is waiting for the user to enter a direct command. If this suddenly appears whilst you are running a program, the program has probably crashed.

real time: a program is said to be operating in 'real time' if the passage of time recorded in a program has a recognizable relationship to the real passage of time.

reinforcement: a term used by educators and psychologists influenced by the behaviourist school of psychology. It refers to the presentation of a reward after the desired response has been made.

relational database: a database in which retrieval involves the formulation of conditions which must be matched (for instance AGE < 12). See also database, hierarchical database.

relational understanding: a term derived from R.R.Skemp. Knowing how to carry out a particular process and understanding why by relating this to more general knowledge. A necessary basis for concept formation. See also instrumental understanding.

response time: the average time taken for the computer to respond to a user's input.

RETURN (also ENTER) : a key on the computer keyboard which, when pressed, tells the computer that you have completed an entry; a function in a BASIC program telling the computer to return to the line following that in which it was diverted to a subroutine.

robot: a computer-controlled device with activating mechanisms, sometimes having sensors.

ROM: read-only memory. Part of a computer's built-in memory store containing permanent data which tells the computer how to work and which cannot be erased by the user.

routine: see subroutine.

routing: guiding the user through an appropriate sequence of frames in a program (see branch, and tree structure).

RUN: a command from the user to the computer which is typed when a program written in a high-level language is to be started.

SAVE, *saving*: a command to the computer which is typed to transfer a program from the main memory to a backing store such as audio cassette or floppy disk.

screen chart: a term sometimes used in the UK to describe a diagram consisting of a series of boxes containing text and graphics drawn up by a program designer to tell the programmer exactly what should appear on the screen at each stage in a program.

screen size: the number of lines and characters per line that a computer can display (several sizes are possible on many microcomputers).

scrolling: the phenomenon whereby when a screen has been filled with the maximum number of lines for its screen size, each additional line of text causes the remainder of the text to rise up the screen by one line, and the previous top line vanishes from immediate view.

serialist approach: sometimes used to refer to a bottom-up strategy (q.v.).

SHIFT: one of the keys on the computer keyboard similar in function to that on a typewriter. It alters the range of characters generated by pressing the alphanumeric keys. For instance, pressing SHIFT may allow you to produce capital letters rather than lower-case letters.

simulation: in computing, exploring the effect of various strategies on pre-defined models of situations, or software comprising such models.

skills: some educationists use this term to refer to what are sometimes implied to be discrete and teachable components of 'competence' in learning (e.g. 'reading skills', 'listening skills', 'thinking skills' and 'information skills'). See also instrumental understanding.

software: in computing, programs and data which are used to control the hardware.

software protection: any technique employed to prevent the unauthorized reproduction of a program.

specification: see program specification.

sprites: a term usually used in connection with the Logo programming language to mean independently moveable screen-images to which the user can assign shape, size, colour and velocity. Sprites provide an easy way to create animated pictures and video-games.

statement: in programming, the term means 'instruction'. PRINT and READ are statements in BASIC.

strategies (sometimes *problem-solving strategies*, or *learning strategies*) : ways of approaching a problem, deliberate or habitual, such as a top-down approach to programming (which involves the initial formulation of an overall plan).

string: a character or a number of connected characters which, although it may contain numbers, is not to be used for calculation and is therefore treated by the computer as a sequence of alphabetical symbols. Usually indicated in a program with the dollar sign ($).

structured programming: a professionally organized style of programming in which the overall design and the intended functions of each part are clear even to a novice amateur programmer.

subroutine: a largely self-contained part of a program dealing with a particular task.

teaching machine: a device for presenting programmed instruction which enjoyed a brief popularity with some teachers in institutional education in the 1960s.

technology: used by this author to refer to all technical means and knowledge, the interests which control them and the uses to which they are put.

telecommunications: the transmission of data by telephone, television, cable, satellite etc., together with the technology and theory of such communications.

telesoftware: computer programs sent by telephone lines, teletext (television signals) or radio. With the appropriate adaptor such programs can be loaded directly into the user's microcomputer.

teletext: a simple computerized information system provided by broadcasting companies for users with the appropriate adaptor on their own television receivers. For example, Ceefax and Oracle in the UK.

top-down approach: a problem-solving strategy in which one begins by devising an overall plan based on a clear goal before breaking the problem down into smaller parts. Such an approach to programming would involve deciding on the structure of the program first, and then creating the necessary sub-procedures. See also bottom-up approach.

transfer problem: in psychology, the issue of whether that which is learned in one context will have any effect on learning in a different context. In educational computing, for example, there is some debate about whether strategies which a child employs in programming will have an effect on her thinking in general.

tree structure: a fundamental framework for structuring the sequence of choices in a program or retrieval system. Prestel is a good example, where the user may proceed from a general index through more specific branches to the particular frame required.

turtle: the name given to a transparent, hemispherical, mobile robot which can be controlled by a microcomputer by means of the programming language called Logo. The term is sometimes also applied to a screen-based image also used for Logo graphics.

user-friendly: an adjective used to describe qualities in a program which make it less remote from the individual user. It may include the display of a user's name on the screen, avoidance of computer jargon, ease of use and a gentle element of humour.

user group: a group of users of a particular computer – largely hobbyists.

validation: the process of testing a program and its associated materials by submission to appropriate specialists (for example, teachers), and by trials in the field of use (for example, classrooms).

VDU: see visual display unit.

verification: checking that a program or datafile is a workable recording, often automatically by use of a specific computer command.

videodisc: a disc which can be used for storing and replaying video film via a television receiver, but which can also be used to store software. Since such software may also control access to both video and other software the 'interactive videodisc' can be a powerful and flexible educational resource.

video monitor: a visual display unit which may or may not be combined with a television receiver. Those specially designed as monitors produce a sharper picture when used with microcomputers.

videotex: Used in the UK to include both viewdata and teletext. In the US usually a synonym for viewdata only.

viewdata: a computerized information retrieval system which uses the telephone network to link users to a database, allowing them to select particular frames, or to choose and order information or goods. Prestel in Britain is one example; Telidon in Canada is another.

visual display unit: a video monitor or a television receiver used to display the user's input and the output from the computer.

volatile memory: internal memory which is cleared of data when the power supply is disconnected.

word-processing, wp: editing, manipulating, storing and printing text on a dedicated word-processor or on a computer running a word-processing program.

word-processor: a dedicated (special-purpose) computer designed at least primarily for word-processing; a computer behaving as a word-processor because of the use of word-processing software (or firmware).

Note Some of these definitions are adapted from the glossary in the author's *Micro-Primer Study Text* (Tecmedia 1982).

Index of Topics

Index of Names

People

Programs